CHURCH UNLIMITED

Youth Work and Mission Today

CHURCH UNLIMITED

Youth Work and Mission Today

Edited by

Nick Shepherd and Jonathan Brant

Matador
9 De Montfort Mews
Leicester LE1 7FW, UK
Tel: (+44) 116 255 9311 / 9312
Email: books@troubador.co.uk
Web: www.troubador.co.uk/matador

ISBN 978-1906221-928

Printed and bound by Cromwell Press, Trowbridge, Wiltshire
Typeset in 11pt Bembo by Troubador Publishing Ltd, Leicester, UK

Matador is an imprint of Troubador Publishing Ltd

CONTENTS

ABOUT THE EDITORS

Jonathan Brant has fifteen years experience of hands-on youth ministry in the US, UK and South America and is currently studying theology. Away from the library he enjoys life with his wife Tricia and son Isaac. Jonathan has written about, and produced resources for, youth ministry for a number of years and is the author of *Youth Alpha*.

Nick Shepherd worked for Youth for Christ for thirteen years, directing its work in Bath and Greenwich. Nick is now a freelance researcher, writer and trainer in youth ministry and mission and edits the *Journal of Youth and Theology*. Nick is married to Bridget and they have young two children.

ABOUT THE CONTRIBUTORS

Gary Bishop works for ALOVE, developing youth and community projects for The Salvation Army across the North West of England and is the author of the book *Darkest England & The Way Back In*. Gary worked for a church in Brighton for ten years before moving to Manchester to work with the EDEN project and plant a church. He now lives in East Manchester with his wife Hannah and their two children.

Pete Brierley is responsible for the youth and children's work at *church.co.uk* and the evening service 'headspace'. Pete has previously been a youth and community worker in Peckham and has set up a community radio station (southsideradio.co.uk) and a youth centre for young people to tackle South London's increasing problems with gangs and antisocial behaviour. Pete is married to Becca and they have one cat called Archie!

Daphne Clifton is a business coach and trainer. She runs her own company, Clifton Consulting, which works hard at building bridges from exclusion to employment. Her estate youth work represents a small part of her business with the rest ranging from motivational speaking to coaching accountants and media executives. Variety is the spice of her life, which she lives to the full!

Jo Dolby is the founder and manager of Bath Youth for Christ's 'One Eighty' project. She is a qualified Youth and Community Worker and has worked in full time youth work for six years.

Fr. Dermott Donnelly is the Director of Youth Services for the R.C. Diocese of Hexham and Newcastle. Ordained for 15 years, most of his priestly ministry has been working with young people. His work includes directing a community of international, young volunteers in evangelism among young people and running a retreat centre. He is author of *How to survive the rest of your Life* – a young person's practical guide.

Tim Evans is CEO of Worth Unlimited, a national Christian charity working with young people on the margins of society. Tim started working with marginalised young people as a volunteer at university. Tim lives with his wife and four foster children on a council estate in Birmingham.

Lucy Hawes is currently the Youth Pastor at St Paul's, Hammersmith. Lucy originally trained in International Business Management and worked at The Daily Telegraph for 2 years before becoming a youth worker. Lucy is currently studying for an MA in Youth Ministry at King's College, London.

Richard James is director of Oxygen (Kingston YFC) a local church inspired charity in South West London that seeks to give young people the opportunity to discover and follow Jesus. Richard grew up in South Wales where he worked as a baker, delivery driver and ship chandler before entering youthwork!

Helen Gatenby has lived in Brunswick, Manchester since 1989 and works for the M13 Youth Project, which specialises in detached youth work with marginalised young people. She is married to Simon, a vicar, and they have two children.

Br. Alan Michael as been an Anglican Franciscan Brother since 1986. He is currently Guardian of the Birmingham Friary and is about to return to his roots in the North East as he takes up the post of Guardian of Alnmouth Friary.

Patrick Regan is the founder and Director of XLP – a charity based in South East London which aims to meet the social, educational and behavioural needs of young people. XLP take lessons, run lunch and after school clubs and orchestrate a variety of community and arts based projects among young people in the inner city. Patrick has also led many mission trips to places like Ghana, South East Asia, St Vincent's and Guyana. Patrick is married to Diane and they have two children, Keziah and Daniel.

Chris Russell is vicar of St. Lawrence Parish Church in Reading, having served his curacy in South East London. Chris is married to Belinda and they have been involved in a variety of youth ministry projects inside and outside the church. Chris recently contributed to *Mission Shaped Youth.*

Nick Russell was a linguist and ICT quality manager, and is a Church Army church planter and youth and community worker on the Ferrier Estate, South London. **Helen Russell** was a district nurse and is now director of the Superkidz Project.

INTRODUCTION

A Church Unlimited

Nick Shepherd and Jonathan Brant

We hear all the time that young people are culturally alienated from the church, but, perhaps, it's the other way around! If you keep up with trends in research into young people's perspectives on religion and spirituality, you will know that evidence is emerging that even the key spiritual questions of the importance and significance of life, let alone life after death, are evaporating from their consciousness.[1] So, how might those involved in youth ministry respond to this 'problem'? How might we go 'beyond the walls' of a comfortable church and engage young people who seem to have little interest in, and perhaps even hostility towards faith?

This is the question that we hope this book will address. There is much that can be written on the topics of mission and ministry to young people from a theoretical perspective (and there are a range of recent books that seek to do this). We have not approached the question in this way (although there is an introductory chapter that sets the scene for thinking about the church's engagement with young people in mission and, at the end, a reflective postscript). Instead, our approach has been to ask people who are doing work beyond the walls of the church to tell their stories.

The story of Christian youth ministry in the UK has always included those who were prepared to go beyond the walls of the church. Paraphrasing the style, if not the specific point of Hebrews 11, we might say that:

In faith, Robert Raikes and Hannah More saw past the present and into the future, working tirelessly alongside unnamed volunteers to attend to those in 'ragged schools'; providing hope, comfort and compassion to those who had helped to build and yet who had missed out on sharing in the riches of their time.

In faith, William Smith, not disheartened by the test and challenge of leading a rowdy and unmanageable boys Sunday school, determined to engage these young men from a tough Glasgow background with a 'sure and steadfast' form of encountering faith that would test and challenge them!

In faith, Josiah Spires, knowing that church services were uninspiring to the young, used his position and influence to make space for children in church and inspired a movement that changed the church.

In faith, David Sheppard, rejecting and yet preserving all he had learned from a privileged education, chose to serve and learn from young people so that the gospel might be seen and understood in a city where others were walking by or talking over the young.

These people all had a better vision of how the world could be (Heb 11:13-16) and they all refused to settle for the standards of the land they lived in. They considered that the Kingdom of heaven was a place of hope and, in faith, they not only rested their lives upon this future, but sought to invest their lives in seeking and praying for this Kingdom to come on earth as it is in heaven. It is the vision of these pioneers (and others) of time gone by that the stories in this book bring up to date.

In this book, we have tried to gather a variety of contributions from a range of perspectives and contexts – urban to sub-urban;

Catholic and evangelical; youth work focussed and youth ministry centred; some based in local churches and others orchestrated by organisations. We do not though propose a theory on how to do youth work beyond the church. This is not a how to book! We hope however that it is a 'why do' book and a 'could do' book – at least that is our intention. The stories we present here give some insight into the inspiration and motivation that has empowered these youth leaders and workers to engage in ambitious and sometimes arduous youth work. We have also asked them to comment on their journey, their struggles and disappointments, their hopes for the future. These are real people! By this I mean that they doubt, try new things and make mistakes. You might feel that they are in someway special or exceptional. They certainly don't feel this way (well, not that they let on!). But while they might not be exceptional we believe they are certainly inspirational. These people, and hundreds of others whose stories we don't have, are our contemporary 'cloud of witnesses'. Their vision and dedication shouldn't make us feel inadequate, but encourage us to 'press on' as they themselves attest to having had to do time and time again.

Most of our contributors are currently 'full-time' youth workers or ministers, but you will see from their stories that this wasn't always the case. We hope that those of you who work with young people in spare moments snatched from busy jobs and families will also recognise yourselves here. Our hope is that whatever your circumstance of ministry you can engage with these stories by reflecting on your sense of call and vision – throughout the book there are questions and spaces for you to write in your reflections and comments.

We will also try to set the scene for our contemporary witnesses, through our first chapter within which Nick Shepherd will discuss how we engage in the practice of youth ministry beyond the walls of the church – under the mission of God. Further, following our contributors stories Jonathan Brant offers a theological postscript to help us mull over some of the issues that might have been raised in the accounts.

At the end of the book there is also a guided section for you to write your story. Though at the time of printing this is only a series of blank pages, we believe that this is possibly the most important chapter. It's your chapter! It's your own place to make a mark and a contribution to the challenge of becoming a church unlimited. In fact, we'd love you to share your story and your ideas with the wider community so that we might spur one another on to try to live out what it means to be the church; a church that engages with our world and especially the world young people experience and enjoy.

The twelve stories that we have brought together in this book are divided into three groups:

First, there are stories of churches connecting, caring and creating communities:

Gary Bishop runs an Eden Project in Openshaw, Manchester. He reflects on the transition from a successful, middle-class, church-based ministry position in Brighton to the challenge of initiating a new project on one of the most deprived housing estates in Britain. The new context demanded new approaches and, even, a new understanding of what mission is, before the team began to see God making good on his promise to redeem and make fruitful this desolate place.

Chris Russell speaks of St. Laurence in Reading, where there is a commitment and vocation to work among non-churched young people and to see them come to faith. Perhaps most importantly, there is a determination not just to try and incorporate these young people into pre-existing expressions of church but to work alongside them to build *new* forms of church.

The hub@church.co.uk is located in London, just south of Big Ben and just north of Brixton. Pete Brierley writes of their mission to bring hope to the young people of the area through a range of popular and innovative activities ranging from football leagues to a local, online radio station. In the spirit of their name, the workers at the "hub" seek to create connections between the young people engaging in these diverse activities and the worshipping community at the centre that is the church.

Bringing this section to a close is Lucy Hawes with the "story so far" of St. Paul's, Hammersmith. Here Christian young people worship together in a "youth church" that has a strong emphasis on mission. They are encouraged to work alongside St. Paul's registered youth charity, W6 Youthworks, in outreaching to the community around them. Churched and unchurched youth have recently come together around a worship event called "The Vibe" which Hawes sees as a first step on a long road of mission to the next generation.

The second group of stories tell of meetings at the margins:

Father Alan Michael, a Franciscan Brother, tells of how he loves to help disaffected youth discover and explore their spiritual being. Working alongside young people in various settings – gangs, prisons and schools – the goal is not, primarily, to connect young people to an institutional church, but to share with them the joys of faith and the possibility of a first-hand relationship with Jesus Christ.

In the next contribution, Nick Russell, Helen Russell and Daphne Clifton share their experiences of working with children and young people (and their families) on the Ferrier Estate. Here the "meetings" take place amidst the pandemonium of the weekly Superkidz extravaganza, in workshops aimed at expanding the life-options of gang members and in week-in-week-out commitment to building relationship with individuals for whom society at large has little hope but for whom God has a purpose and a plan. This account is a little larger than the others since it is actually the story of two projects gathered around the same church.

Jo Dolby is the leader of One Eighty, an outreach to the skater subculture that grew out of the desire to show this sometimes despised and rejected group that they are loved, honoured and accepted by Christians and by God. As the name suggests, Dolby and her co-workers are desperate to present a relevant Gospel and see young people turn through 180 degrees and return to God.

Helen Gatenby has lived and worked for eighteen years on an inner-urban housing estate in Brunswick, just south of Manchester city-centre. Since 1995 she has led the M13 project which works in partnership with YFC and local churches. The key point of contact and the prime location for the work is actually on the streets where the workers take the time to "walk alongside" the young people as they confront the challenges of life – watch out for Gatenby's excellent "golf caddy" analogy!

Tim Evans lives with his wife and family on a council estate in Birmingham. They have a vision for providing a level of support for at risk young people that goes far beyond that provided by typical social services or residential care. In short, they want to provide these young people with an experience of *family*. It is only in this kind of environment that Evans believes these young people can come to experience the full expression of God's *Shalom* peace.

Richard James tells the story of an outreach with a distinctly *sub*-urban feel. The journey began when local residents began to speak to James's YFC team about the problems caused by groups of young people hanging around and making a nuisance of themselves. The team came up with the radical plan of confronting antisocial behaviour with *social* behaviour. Volunteers would pray and then head out into the night armed with hot chocolate, biscuits and, sometimes, cakes baked by local church members. Conversations started, relationships developed and Urban Nites was born.

The final stories are about resourcing and reaching, the essential roles often taken on by para-church organisations:

Patrick Reagan tells of the remarkable growth of XLP, a charity with a story which began with a one-off visit to a local school, but eventually spread through Peckham, onto South London and even beyond (to West Africa!). This schools-based outreach uses mentoring, lessons, lunchtime clubs, and talent contests to bring a message of hope to young people. XLP have a God-given passion to see communities transformed and for young people whom society has written off given the chance to lead "normal" lives.

Father Dermot Donnelly tells of how the Hexham and Newcastle YOuth Ministry Team grew out of the Catholic Charismatic Renewal Movement in the seventies. It has flourished and now has its own Youth Village and a threefold strategy: bringing international young people to carry out missions in the UK; utilising a retreat centre where young people can experience the love of God; and, perhaps most importantly, acting as a catalyst to facilitate, support and encourage holistic youth ministry in the parishes of the diocese.

The final story on the book is that of LCET – Luton Churches Education Trust. Chris Curtis articulates the journey his team found themselves on to develop a youth ministry that could communicate the gospel in ways which made sense to young people with no experience of the church – those who wrestled with problems at home, found reading difficult and struggled to listen to an adult speaker for very long – but that would also equip and empower these young people to be able to express their spirituality for themselves.

Note

1. See Savage, Sara B. (2006). Making Sense of Generation Y : The World View of 15- to 25-Year-Olds. London, Church House and Rankin, Phillip (2005).

CHAPTER ONE

Youth Ministry and Mission

Nick Shepherd

A church unlimited in mission, not limited by evangelism

In this chapter I discuss some basic theological premises that pertain to a vision of 'church unlimited'. There are many areas and avenues for discussion around the topic of what it means to be church circulating the blogs and bookstalls, but I haven't got much to add to that. There are numerous theological considerations to contend with; to examine what the church is and whether it is possible to 'get beyond its walls', but we haven't got the space to go into that. Instead, I want to look at one facet of the churches engagement with young people beyond the church – why? Literally, why bother? Surely if we focus on doing our job properly with young people in the church then that will be enough? If they are firmly rooted in faith and the church, then they will do the job of mission among their peers (which we can support). However, back in 1997, Pete Ward provided a more than adequate assessment of the problems inherent in simply relying on re-enforcing church based ministry as a strategy for renewal in mission in his seminal book *Youthwork and the Mission of God.*[1]

To oversimplify his case, church youth ministry is important, but it isn't enough: our church culture gets in the way. In fact the world we live in, and the gap between the life of the church and our society, means that church youth ministry is a problem in its own right that needs a specific focus – church based youth ministry. We need to develop specialists and leaders to minister to young people who have grown up in the church, support and nurture them and help the church grow from the 'inside-out'. However, this will only ever result in small numbers of young people who already have some connection and compatibility hearing and responding to the gospel. So, we ought to be more proactive in mission – working from the 'outside-in' to enable the gospel to become known within the cultural groups that young people occupy outside the church. We can do this through relational youth work.

Pete Ward helped to popularise the term 'relational youth work'. I won't summarise his rich and still relevant theory here, so if you have not read *Youthwork and the Mission of God* I urge you to! Unfortunately in my view, many people who have adopted the term relational youth work to describe their work haven't caught the subtleties of the agenda for youth ministry that Ward presented in his book and that I believe our contributors in this book represent. This is because, for most of us, we have inherited or been schooled into a particular view of mission, a view of mission which is centred on the notion of evangelism and as such we can miss the heart of what relational youth work is all about. It is this particular aspect of youth ministry outside the church we want to focus on in this opening chapter – moving from evangelism to mission.

Evangelism and the church

Much reflection and writing on evangelism has often tended to take pragmatic approaches to the subject, focussing on methodology – 'how to's in telling testimony and putting on events. This approach though leads to an overemphasis on technique and style that does not enquire sufficiently into the theological issues of both the context and practice of evangelism.[2] Indeed, a focus on method might also have reduced the richness in the understanding of evangelism itself. This is perhaps indicated by our need to 'invent' terms such as *'pre-evangelism'* and *'re-evangelism'* to describe work that is considered important in making contact with, supporting and nurturing people; but somehow falls short of 'evangelism proper'.[3] Similarly, there is some evidence that by elevating the role of evangelism in church life, other activity can appear devalued or subordinate to it:[4] pastoral visiting becomes an opportunity to invite someone to Alpha; an assembly or an open youth club is a place where the youth service or 'mission event' can be advertised etc.

Yet, whilst being ready to bear witness when asked about our faith (cf. 1 Peter 3:5), such a focus on opportunity and technique is not present in the New Testament. In *The Provocative Church*, Graham Tomlin (now director of the St. Paul's Theological Centre in London) points to a way of approaching evangelism which is more consistent with the teaching of the New Testament. To encapsulate what he says, I draw attention to a brief postscript study on Ephesians. Tomlin addresses why evangelism is not highlighted more specifically in the New Testament as an activity of the church as because:

> *"By and large, the letter of Ephesians doesn't tell Christians to make a priority of getting out there and evangelizing. It does tell them to love each other, to learn new ways of relating in families and at work, to gain freedom from damaging obsessions, and a healthy scepticism towards the idols of the age. It tells them to develop a completely new way of living."*[5]

Living such lives was seen as being the critical way through which the gospel would be observed and encountered and this still holds true for today. Our task of being church has the paramount calling of being the gospel community. We are a people who have experienced the compassion of a God who does not count our failings as a barrier to his love, nor our past and often ongoing rejection of him as cause to be dismissed from his presence and purposes. Indeed, because of Christ we experience the opposite, a God who continually reaches out to us through His spirit and word. We experience his grace, we receive measures of healing and wholeness and we are counted among his people – his family. This is the gospel. We reciprocate to the gift of this gospel in the worship offered through our lives as well as our larynxes (Romans 12) and this has to be central to our vision for church youth ministry. First, our lives together as church ought to be ordered and focussed on trying to be God's people – learning what we can from each other, forgiving what we ought of each other and encouraging one another through our common and personal struggles.

The church is both a picture of the problem of being human and an image of the future of our complete redemption. This is one reason why the church is the key agent of God's mission. The church doesn't only carry the message of the gospel, the church is where the gospel is enacted, embodied and encountered. In effect we are all charged with being a Royal Priesthood (1 Peter 2:9) ministering the grace of the gospel first to each other and hopefully as well to those around us in other spheres of our lives. This has always been the way God has chosen to act in mission – he chooses a family, a people, a nation, a family of people from all nations to be His and he commits to being with them, to aid them, to heal them and all he asks is that they stay faithful to him, that they seek Him when they are in distress and that they serve Him by showing others the justice and joy of living a life in the way He directs.

Youth ministry is one particular out-working of how the church attempts to remember and pass on this way of living. Now, fine preaching rhetoric I know, but we all know that the reality of being church and of engaging in youth ministry isn't that easy and yes, there are lots of appropriate questions about the way we try to organise our lives together as God's 'family' and how we communicate and share this life with others. However, my main concern here is to suggest that church youth ministry doesn't exist just because there are young people in a church who need to be distracted or detained from leaving by creating structures and styles to reach and keep! Nor does it exist simply to recruit new young people into the church. Youth ministry exists (or at least ought to) to enable young people inside and outside the church to encounter and embody the pain, joy and hope of living as God's people and to respond to a call to participate in ministering this hope to one another and world around them. However, if our churches don't connect as Ward and many others[6] contest – we need to do something about it! We need to go beyond the walls of the church.

However, sharing the good news of the gospel with others is not a simple transmission of knowledge about God, it is also part of the way 'the gospel' becomes reality to us! Through sharing our story, our hope, our lives we actually learn more about the God we serve – through the struggles we face in overcoming our own fears, through the experiences of acceptance or rejection we encounter, through the insight or inspiration we gain from sharing in one another's struggles and successes. It is, as Andrew Walker puts it, "by telling the story that the message becomes the gospel"[7]. This holds true for our lives together as the church, but it is even more so the case when we seek to engage with those outside the church. However, in order to enter into such a process of living and experiencing the gospel, I believe we need to ironically reduce the emphasis we often place on evangelism as the primary task of the church.

Encountering the gospel through mission

In a view of mission that supports church unlimited, I do not want to dispense with evangelism *per se*, but rather the mode of understanding evangelism as the be all and end all of mission. Contemporary missiological literature identifies a way of doing this through the notion of the mission of God (*missio Dei*).[8] A cornerstone to m*issio Dei* is that mission originates with God. God's mission is, as biblical scholar and Missiologist Christopher Wright outlines, the story of the bible.[9] God has and is always working to make himself known throughout time, from creation to the culmination of redemption in a new heaven and a new earth, but God is the author and director of this story:[10] mission is not an activity initiated by the church.[11] The church, as God's people, have been graciously included and involved in God's activity. God's mission is to call his creation to reflect his attributes and character, to re-align ourselves with him. As such, seeking justice and equality; challenging poverty and slavery; seeking to gift human dignity through education and meaningful employment are all to be seen in relationship to God as creator and to his nature of righteousness, compassion and grace not 'good ideas of ours for human society based on the bible.' The church involved in *missio Dei* has the calling of reflecting the attributes of God's character (which we discern partly through biblical witness) to our society and societal structures. Mission is not simply working up a marketing platform through which we recruit new members!

Christian youth work has been at the forefront of developing work grounded in *missio Dei* for some time. In the rest of this chapter I want to explore why rooting our practice in the mission of God provides a clear rationale for working with young people beyond the church. To do this I want to cover three areas. Firstly, that the mission of God involves recognition that the church is sent by God into His world to serve and, second, that we serve by seeking and enacting His Kingdom. Third, our service, our part in enacting the Kingdom also includes the challenge to call all people to account for the way we act in God's world and to challenge others (and it has to be said, remind ourselves) to re-orientate their lives under God through entering His Kingdom.

The mission of God involves being sent

Perhaps the starting point for appreciating being sent is in understanding how God himself sent himself. Mission actually means 'sending' and it is critical in this to reflect on God's nature – love.

> *"God is love. God showed how much he loved us by sending his only Son into the world so that we might have eternal life through him. This is real love. It is not that we loved God, but that he loved us and sent his Son as a sacrifice to take away our sins" (1 John 4:8ff-10).*

The church is sent in continuation of this demonstration of love: "*as [the Father] sent me into the world, I am sending them into the world*" (John 17:18). This sending is also linked to the sending of the Holy Spirit, the counsellor, to lead and guide believers and help us in the difficulties we will face in remaining in Christ in a hostile world (John 14:6-18, 26-27, 15:26-27). However, beyond this empowerment of the church God himself is also active by His Spirit: "*He will convince the world of its sin and of God's righteousness*" (John 16:8)

Catch that – it is God that does the convincing not us! This brings an important balance to our activity as participants in God's mission. Firstly, our motivation must mirror God's – love. Secondly, though the church is sent in mission, we are dependent on the empowering of the Spirit. Thirdly, we can expect God to be active by His Spirit outside of our activities and understanding.

Sending validates a range of ministries. Youth ministry is aptly called ministry and not simply 'youth evangelism' because it engages young people in the church and wider community in a variety of supportive, pastoral *and* evangelistic activities. Rooting such ministry in *missio Dei* provides a unifying theme across all activity, as opposed to seeing certain activities as 'contact' opportunities, some as 'service' opportunities and yet others as 'evangelistic' opportunities. Further, through *missio Dei,* activities such as reading support, mentoring and health education have validity in their own right.

John Stott famously declared that evangelism and social action are the two components of mission.[12] This was most likely intended to provide a synthesis between the ideas of 'declaring' and 'demonstrating' the gospel. However, in doing so Stott inadvertently identified a tangible separation between these components. Because of theological arguments about which aspects of mission were important, attitudes were fracturing such that different groups say, "You do the social action, we'll do evangelism; together that's mission". *Missio Dei* lessens the strongly dualistic theological underpinning behind this; namely that salvation is a 'vertical' relationship between people and God with eternal implications that have 'horizontal' implications in how one lives life now.[13] In this regard proclamation (and response) was the means to satisfying the vertical relationship, with any action taken in working socially or physically as a mere indication, or evidencing, of the greater liberation that is found through 'faith'. In contrast, *missio Dei* suggests that mission ought to be holistic – ministering to a person's total need and to their communities. Verbal articulation is an important aspect of this, but actions are vital as well. This is evidenced by Luke 7:19 – 22, where the writer highlights that John's disciples were told by Christ that the evidence that he was the Messiah was found in what they *saw* in addition to what they *heard.*[14]

As I have said, *missio Dei* also introduces an appreciation of God's activity outside of the church. In the mission of God, God may have a role for other institutions, such as schools, work places and families. Each of these areas of life can be places where God is bringing the Kingdom to fruition as much as they can be areas were people experience damage from sin. With this in mind, partnership working in mission has totally different connotations. There was many a time around a Connexions board room table that I had to remind myself that I had an opportunity to provoke and pray for this structure to not be simply a government initiative but also a potential instrument of the Kingdom. As such, mission requires a dialogue with others in these areas of common life. This understanding supports Christian vocational involvement in schools, in the Youth Service – in providing resources that support the common good and in developing projects of common interest between churches and groups in the community, not least of which young people themselves.[15] But what of evangelism? Here, there are different options from different traditions, but evangelism for all orthodox Christians (despite what our prejudices might inform) is a crucial aspect of mission.

A 'liberal approach' is to suggest that engagement in mission is such that the challenge of the gospel can be integrated into dialogue activities through which the church may discover fresh ways in which to communicate, understand and respond to the gospel.[16] This reasoning contends that our understating of the gospel may be rightly challenged, broadened or redefined by this dialogue with culture[17]. This is vital to consider when we think about youth ministry and mission. We are not the source of hope; we are not the saviours of the young people we might encounter. We can provoke interest in God, but we can also encounter issues we can do nothing about! This journey with young people may be a way that we encounter the gospel further, through a sense of our own powerlessness.

From an evangelical perspective, engagement through dialogue and common activities provokes a sense of interest or desire for God that will lead to people to become interested in the gospel story.[18] This too is a helpful perspective: we are called to make clear the 'hope to which we have been called'; seeing our task as being sent to get involved in His mission is an affirmation that God chooses to use His church to convey who He is. The church is first and foremost a 'missional' community, charged with the task of declaring and demonstrating the reign and rule of God.[19] This task is expressed in a broad engagement with our society, but also has particular significance to the church as the '*gospelled community*', where people see, hear and experience this story.[20]

For youth ministry this sets two important benchmarks and a wide parameter of possibilities. First, our actions amongst young people ought to be guided by seeking God's Kingdom throughout our society and, second, we ought to be focussed on somehow enabling people to encounter an expression of the church through which they can further encounter and in deed interpret God's kingdom. It is to this complex calling I now turn.

The mission of God involves seeking the kingdom of God

Missio Dei is heavily identified with seeking the Kingdom – seeking God's rule.[21] Though the centrality of the Kingdom is evident in Jesus' teaching and ministry, the enactment of the Kingdom is not immediately identifiable. In addition to difficulty in identifying what constitutes the presence of the Kingdom, its arrival is held in an 'eschatological tension': it is both present now and yet to come.

These paradoxes prompt questions as to the purpose of the church's involvement in mission. Is it to enact the principles we understand God's Kingdom to contain now, through improving social conditions for instance, or to 'save people' so that they may experience God's Kingdom when it comes in full? Howard Snyder analyses these tensions and suggests, rather conveniently perhaps, that they remain in 'the mystery of the Kingdom'.[22] He does this by postulating that if we analyse the biblical teaching on the Kingdom of God, there are several clear tensions – like that of the 'present now and yet to come' paradox I have already mentioned. He offers six differing polarities which are illustrated opposite.

These polarities relate to genuine tensions such as that the Kingdom is a treasure that an individual may find (Matt 13:44) and into which someone must be born again to experience (John3:3), but it is also a feast that we are called to share and invite those who others might not wish to dine with (Luke 13:29). The Kingdom is not equal to the church, but the church is declared to have the 'keys to the Kingdom' (Matt 16:19). Another common tension we have

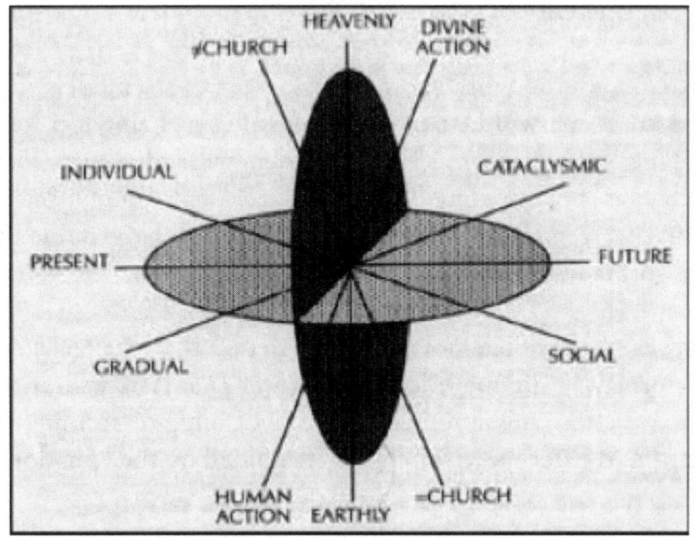

Figure 1: Snyder's six polarities that establish the 'mystery of the Kingdom' (Snyder 2001)

already mentioned is that the Kingdom is both rightly understood as God's to achieve, but something that people must seek to find (Matt 6:33) and where we are 'Gods fellow workers' (Col 4:11). From all this Snyder argues that:

> *"Theologies of the Kingdom that dissolve these tensions, opting wholly for one side or the other are to that degree unbiblical".*[23]

Even where this has not been done to exclusion, these polarities form a matrix within which there are distinct 'models' of the Kingdom – which in the book Snyder evaluates from his observations of different church tendencies and interpretations. However, to a degree Snyder's approach is that none of use will ever be totally right in our take. To a certain extent this validates flexibility over the way in which God's rule is extended, entered and fulfilled, but it also provides a critique against biases in practice; one component of action should not be seen as being a more valid activity of mission than another.

Christian youth workers will disagree over models of the Kingdom. Some will be perceived by others as being too focussed on solving social problems and still others will judge some forms of ministry as not tackling the real issues and simply seeking a spiritual conversion which does little to bring the genuine impact of the gospel to bear in people's lives.

However, this should not lead to a denial that evangelism itself does not have a unique role within *missio Dei*. As I will discuss in the next section, mission includes both a calling to account and an invitation to enter more full into a life guided by the Kingdom.

The mission of God includes calling people to account

A weakness of the Kingdom focus in *missio Dei* is that it could create "an anything goes approach to mission".[24] Evangelism perhaps has a role in keeping our mission honest.

For some, evangelism is a distinct task of the church from that of mission:

> *"Evangelism is the spreading of the good news by proclamation, whereas mission is the outflow of the love of God in and through life, word and deed."*[25]

However, such a separation is inadequate. Evangelism needs to be involved in a wider sense of mission because 'the gospel' is not easily reducible to a scheme of ethics or set of doctrines that can be presented.[26] The gospel, as the American biblical scholar Walter Brueggemann argues, is better understood as an ongoing drama between God, creation and humanity. This drama has three scenes:

1. God's decisive action
2. The announcement which mediates that victory
3. The lived appropriation of that victory

He identifies that this motif is evident throughout the biblical narrative and is not (as I have already discussed) exclusively an activity of the church.[27] Further, Brueggemann argues that in this drama, practical and not merely proclamational, aspects of mission can be evangelistic:

> *"[Evangelism] may be proclaimed boldly by action and risky intervention where the power of death invades common life. Thus an act which embodies the news may be regarded as an announcement".*[28]

However, to combat the tension in the purpose of such actions being missed or misunderstood, evangelism also contends with the need to identify an inherent challenge deeply embedded in this notion of the gospel as an ongoing drama, which, as Andrew Walker suggests, is that,

> *"The church is the community that continues to participate in this drama and to insist that this drama is the definitional account of its life in the world."*[29]

Engaging in the broad task of mission does not devalue the place and challenge of evangelism; but does require it to be understood as only able to be expressed through engaging in the broad task of mission.

Yet, we ought not rush to recruit! Ann Morrisy, the recent chair of the Church Commission on Urban Life and Faith, helpfully identifies three domains to mission – the explicit, the foundational and the vocational. The explicit domain is where people join churches. This is a good thing, but within this explicit call to respond to the gospel there is often an implicit requirement to adopt the views and practices of the denomination or theological basis of that particular church. Like Ward, she sees this as a problem because, whilst most people in churches don't see it, the way we do church – our language, symbols and customs – are thoroughly unfamiliar to the outsider. This does not mean that in time such things won't become meaningful and helpful in a person's faith, just that at the outset they might actually be off putting. To combat this, Morrisy suggests that the church also has a foundational domain to undertake, if in our mission we are to be fruitful in our (or other churches) explicit call for people to respond to the gospel. A foundational domain to mission requires us to engage people in a patient and unforced manner such that "people establish the possibility of God existing 'out there', thus providing the foundation to enable movement from God 'out there' to a God that exists in people's hearts and minds".[30] She goes further however, to suggest that we also ought to consider a vocational domain to mission – "encouraging and enabling people to express discipleship, regardless of whether they are Christian." Such a strategy is founded on the hope that when people join in as participants in the mission of God, it can prove to be "a route to faith and not just an expression of faith".[31]

Such an idea might turn on its head our classic ways of perceiving evangelism and discipleship, but it isn't perhaps too different from the way in which Jesus and the early church operated. We need to take heed of this as we consider how to invite and integrate young people to participate in God's story. For Morrisy, a conversation pathway is more messy and muddled than a classic *believe, belong, behave* pathway; and even more radical than simply rearranging these markers of faith commitment. Similar understanding is found within catholic approaches to evangelism. Anglican priest Stephen Cottrell identifies the following cycle as a foundation for catholic evangelism.[32]

The dimension of nurture is linked with the notion of 'accompanying someone on their faith journey' which has strong

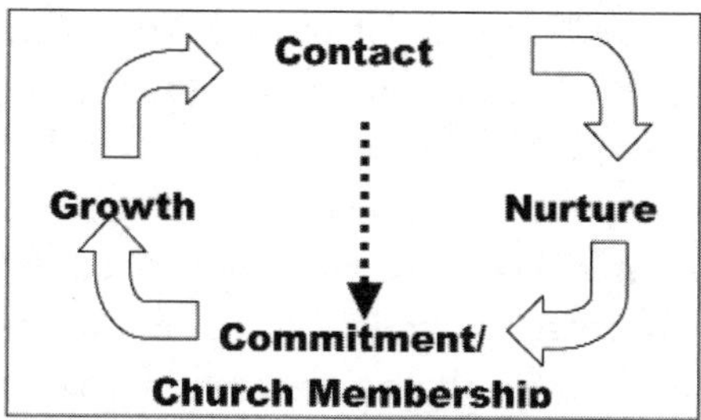

Figure 2: An accompanied journey model of evangelism (Cottrell, 1998)

connections with the catechistic tradition. However, re-reading this with Morrisy might help us consider a way in which a faith journey begins outside of the church. In this, it is particularly important to note that Cottrell also argues that circumventing the cycle (the dotted line in figure above, is counter productive and an 'artificial' task that devalues the gospel and the person: evangelism "must never be satisfied with anything less than the making of disciples."[33] Conversion is envisaged as a process with many decision (or crisis) points – and commitment to Christ is central. As people encounter the telling, or enactment, of the gospel story, the intention is to initiate them further into that story so that it becomes their defining view of the world.

The idea of catechism, from a historical perspective, is a helpful provocation for modern evangelism. In this process the *catechumate* had to spend three years in preparation before they were baptised into the faith as 'a believer'[34]. I don't have time to address this here, but perhaps three years of continual contact with a relational youth work project is the bare minimum we should consider giving people when we ask them to think about church!! This may give an indication of the process that is actually required to help people more fully appropriate the decisions they are making and, following Morrisy, being able to participate themselves in the mission of God could fundamentally influence this understanding for the better.

All these avenues and aspects of evangelism, within mission, are crucial to being a church unlimited. Our role in mission is unlimited. God might call us to minister in the most unlikely context, partnering with the most unlikely agency. However, to achieve this unlimited vocation we might need to limit our own view of our importance as well as limit our immediate desire to 'evangelise'. Yet, as a result, we may find that we are actually enabled (and empowered) to demonstrate and declare more adequately the richness of the gospel and the significance of the Kingdom. In short, Youth ministry, as I will end by summarising, belongs in the mission of God.

Youth Ministry and the Mission of God

Youth ministry that locates itself within *missio Dei* is humble, honest and holistic. This humility is seen through genuine dialogue and seeing the possibility that others, who may not even profess a faith, may demonstrate values that we would recognise as those of the Kingdom. It is the attitude of being sent in love that genuinely serves, rather than one that 'uses' needs in the community to serve our own evangelistic agenda.

Honesty, however, means that whilst engaging in such dialogue we ought not and need not hide our beliefs but be open with these positions, even where that brings us into disagreement or limits our engagement. Honesty too is applied to our own limitations in our knowledge of the gospel and how this should be interpreted and lived: we may learn through our engagement with young people fresh interpretations and perspectives.

A holistic approach to youth ministry does not relegate the value of serving young people's current physical, social and educational needs as immaterial to the task of mission, but it also means that we strive to work out how the gospel challenges both the ways in which our communities treat young people and the ways in which young people might be maltreating themselves or others.

Contemporary youth ministry is at the forefront of developing such mission. However, this is not without significant challenges and it is to these that we will now turn attention as we hear stories from practitioners at the forefront of 'being the church without walls'.

Notes

1 Ward, Pete (1997). Youthwork and the Mission of God. London, SPCK. Publsihed in America under the title God at the Mall, Hendrickson
2 Abraham W, The Logic of Evangelism, (London: Hodder & Stoughton, 1989) p.2
3 Bosch (1996) p.412
4 Tomlin G, The Provocative Church (London: SPCK, 2002) p.66
5 Tomlin G, The Provocative Church, p.172.
6 For instance the recent report Mission Shaped Youth (London: Church House, 2007)
7 Walker (1996) p.11
8 Bosch (1996) p.370
9 Wright C, The Mission of God: Unlocking the Bible's grand narrative (Nottingham: IVP, 2006) p.28
10 Kirk (1999) p.27
11 Kirk (1999) p.26
12 Bosch (1996) p.412
13 Donald McGavran cited in Bosch (1996) p.398
14 Watson D, I Believe in Evangelism (I Believe Green M, ed.), (London: Hodder & Stoughton, 1976) p.28
15 Reader J, Local Theology – Church and community in dialogue, (London: SPCK, 1994)
16 Saxbee A, Liberal Evangelism: A flexible response to 'the decade' (London: SPCK, 1994) p.43
17 ibid p.40-55
18 Tomlin G, The Provocative Church (London: SPCK, 2002) p.150
19 Bosch (1996) p.372
20 Walker (1996) p.28
21 Kirk (1999) p.27
22 Snyder H, Models of the Kingdom (Eugene USA: Wipf & Stock, 1991) p.16
23 ibid p.17

24 Kirk (1999) p.25
25 Metropolitan Mar Osthathios cited in Abraham (1989) p.42
26 Abraham (1996) p.11-12
27 Brueggemann W, Biblical Perspectives on Evangelism: Living in a three storied universe (Nashville USA: Abingdon, 2000) p.22-25
28 Brueggemann (2000) p.40
29 Walker (1996)
30 Morisy, Ann (2004). Journeying Out : A New Approach to Christian Mission. London ; New York, Morehouse. p.174-176
31 Morrisy (2004) p.218
32 Cottrell (1998) p.23
33 Cottrell (1998) p.19-26
34 Bradshaw, Early Christian Worship: A basic introduction to ideas and practice (London: SPCK, 1996), p.8 & p.25

Stories to Inspire and Imitate

CHURCHES CONNECTING, CARING AND CREATING COMMUNITY

CHAPTER TWO

Open Church in Openshaw

Eden Project, Manchester

Gary Bishop

I had been a youth worker for ten years; four as a volunteer, two as a student and a further four as a full time employee of my church in Brighton. Those years were hugely fulfilling with many things to celebrate, not least my own personal and spiritual growth throughout the process. Looking back, although at times the work was very demanding there were some fairly easy victories for me; the challenge of stemming the flow of young people who had been flooding out of the church doors for years was one that I relished. Giving them something to stay for; some positive encouragement, opportunities to participate, some accessible teaching, some valuable relationships, some fun times all seemed simple enough and at least slowed the tide of young people vacating the pews. As we increasingly managed to hold on to a good number of the young people from church families we also saw a little bit of growth as those young people introduced friends and others joined through our outreach activities. This, of course, won much praise from the many parents who were longing for their kids to stay in church and find faith for themselves. Many young people did find that faith and along with my fantastic team I enjoyed the good will that was generated towards us for the solid, successful church youth work that we were doing.

Then my personal journey took a very different turn, through a series of events – some deeply spiritual and others profoundly ordinary – I found myself making the long trip north to Manchester to face the daunting prospect of starting an Eden project in Openshaw, one of the most deprived housing estates in Britain. The transition did not happen without a great deal of struggle and there was a very great sense of calling without which I never would have had the courage to make this move. My attitude at that time was as arrogant as it was naïve – I'd think; surely all young people are fundamentally the same! How different could it be to what I knew? No doubt once I flashed my evangelical credentials and provided the answers to all life's questions this place will be middle class and charismatic in no time.

Then reality began to dawn. The day I moved to Manchester I was given an A-Z and a set of keys to the old Salvation Army building that had been closed for a good few years. I had no church, no team, no house, no friends, no program and no idea where to start. I remember thinking, 'What if no one comes? What if this thing is a total failure? Then everyone will know I've been blagging this whole youth work thing all this time.'

Do you ever feel that your inadequacies might be 'found out' when you are confronted with a new challenge? What are appropriate and positive ways you can respond to these fears?

Soon a few people did start to come, a team gathered and we all found houses in the small terraced houses on the Toxteth Street Estate which remains one the of the toughest parts of the community. A great team of volunteers joined me – an accountant, a teacher, sales assistants, students, nurses, a solicitor, youth workers – but most importantly each one had a vision for their life and a passion to see this community transformed. When the original team of 16 gathered, we realised that each one of us had what you might call a sense of 'calling' or 'vocation' about being in Openshaw at this time – we were on a mission.... a quest.... an adventure and our vision was transformation.

In the early months of the Eden project we spent a lot of time on the streets of Openshaw. Most, if not all, of us had never really done this before and it was pretty scary at times but two or three nights a week we would go out in teams meeting young people on their territory. After a while of consistent presence on the streets we made contact with just about every young person in our community and soon earned the reputation of being 'The God Squad'. There was certainly no lack of interest from young people; they were really keen to get know us, often knocking the doors of team members, coming into our hall during the week or on Sundays when we were worshipping together, and our staff team were regularly in and out of the local high schools doing lessons and mission weeks with the World Wide Message Tribe (as it was) and we soon started running activities for the young people as we saw the need.

One day as I was driving along a side street with my wife in the car we saw a large crowd of young people from our youth club. Wanting to be friendly and do a good youth work thing, I stopped to say hi. We both wound down our windows expecting some polite conversation but in a second there were bodies all over the car, a hand grabbing at the keys dangling from the ignition, two boys prostrate on the bonnet with faces pressed hard against the windscreen, another two pounding above our heads, and at the passenger window a hand was trying to prise a baseball cap from Hannah's head. Panic set in – what should we do? Driving off would be potentially dangerous to the young people; staying still could result in all kinds of damage to our car not to mention its terrified driver and passenger; all my good youth work training had drummed into me that no physical contact is allowed so manhandling the limbs that protruded through the windows was definitely out of the question. Slowly and deliberately I began to edge the car forward and to our relief the bodies began to alight the car bonnet and roof, but still a hand tried to remove the cap. As we edged away and the would-be thief realised that a neat pony tail was foiling his assault he spat fully in Hannah's face, yelled a string of obscenities and removed his hand.

Clearly we were entering another paradigm in terms of youth work. The days of cozy pizza nights, glitzy youth worship events, one to one discipleship programs, overseas mission trips and retreat weekends which I had enjoyed (perhaps more than any young person who attended) were gone. The quick wins and easy victories of my past experience would not translate into this new world. This was Manchester, this was the inner city and this was home. Very quickly I began to realise what a privileged upbringing I had had and how a world exists within the shores of The United Kingdom that I had never had cause to notice from the comfort of suburbia; a world where the pressures, issues and concerns of young people are very different to those that I had encountered before. Of course, young people growing up in wealthier suburbs faced very real challenges too but perhaps I could relate to those more easily because they were closer to my own experience of adolescence, whereas living and working in a community which owns a whole different set of problems felt very alien to me.

During the seven years which have passed since I moved to Openshaw I have learned many things, not just in the practice of youth work, but things about myself, about the world and about God. I've gained a very different understanding of what mission is. I used to think that mission was all about evangelism and converts; I used to think that my goal for each young person was plain and simple conversion and my programs were correspondingly based around that assumption. Every week I would find a new and creative way to communicate the gospel, as I understood it, and lay down a challenge for people to become Christians. Once commitments were made there would be an intensive one to one discipleship program which taught the convert how they should live in their new found faith.

Whilst there is still a desire within me to see young people embark on their own spiritual journey and ultimately have their relationship with their creator restored I now understand that God's mission is far broader than evangelism.

I've come to believe that God's desire for each and every person is to see us restored in our relationships with creation, with one another and with him; to see us fulfilling the potential that he has given each one of us; to see us living a full life with dignity and honour. This broad view of the Christian mission has informed the work that we do amongst young people in Openshaw and helped us to see real value in every piece of work which helps and supports young people through tough times – even if it doesn't directly result in conversion. Our projects and programs have generally grown out of a need that has become apparent in the community.

For example, I got talking to a lad one night and our conversation clearly bought home to me the issues that many of our young people have surrounding education.

> 'What school are you at?'
> *'I'm not'*
> 'What do you mean?'
> *'I don't go to school.'*
> 'Have you been suspended or something?'
> *'No'*
> 'What then?'
> *'I just don't go – OK?'*
> 'OK… so why not?'
> *'Didn't like it'*
> 'Oh, what didn't you like about it?'
> *'All the teachers 'n' that, they were always picking on me, saying I was causing trouble so I thought – sack it. So I went home and told me mam I'm not going to school no more.'*
> 'What did she say?'
> *'She said I have to go, it's the law. But they can't make me go can they? What are they going to do – drag me there in handcuffs?*
> 'So what are you going to do for the rest of your life?'
> *'Dunno.'*
> 'How old are you now?'

'Eleven'

This conversation happened 5 years ago and the lad never returned to school. His story could be heard dozens of times from the young people of our estate.

There are all kinds of reasons why many young people in our community find school a huge challenge: there are few role models who have excelled in our local schools, lots of the young people have behavioural or attention difficulties, many live in over crowded houses where there is no space to do homework, many are carers for sick or addicted parents who don't care whether they attend or not. The school system as it stands is not capable of teaching a huge proportion of the children of our community. Because of these and many more issues huge numbers of young people drop out of the school system and join the NEET category (Not in Education Employment or Training).

Are you able to identify a particular need that confronts the young people in your location and to which you could offer some part of the solution?

So what is our Christian response to a need like this? There are many possibilities but we have initiated a few small things as opportunities arose.

Firstly, we were able to start a breakfast club and an after-school homework club in the local high school. Here was an opportunity for young people to do any work that needed to be completed and have access to an interested adult who could discuss any challenges they might be facing at school or at home.

When the school realised the value of this intervention they invited us to pilot a mentoring program for pupils whose performance had dropped off for some reason. One of our youth workers Liz recalls; 'There was one lad who was referred to me on the verge of expulsion for repeatedly disrupting lessons. Whenever I met him he was so calm and sweet I could hardly believe what the teachers were telling me about his behaviour. As I listened to him talk it was obvious that he was being bullied and at certain points in the day his temper would just erupt. We tried our best to curb the bullying and created some space for him to chill when he got agitated and that enabled him to carry on with school and achieve well rather than being expelled.' After about 2 years the school made the mentoring program a mainstream service.

Following the success of the work in the school we were able to develop a mentoring program that runs from our church building. Having acquired 'Centre' status with Awards & Qualifications Alliance (AQA) we are now offering the unit award scheme to all kinds of young people. This gives them training, experience and accreditation in a diverse range of subjects such as IT, cooking, event planning, prejudice and anger management to name just a few.

To my mind this is mission; helping young people to achieve their potential, giving them a chance to succeed, working with whole families to rebuild relationships. There is, of course, much more that can be done and there is no shortage of need but these are some of our efforts to help young people in the area of education. Results have been mixed: many of the guys and girls we have worked with over the years have responded really well and their lives have been transformed by the small interactions that we have made; others have still slid off the radar of society and are at best destined for unfulfilled lives of unemployment and social isolation or, at worst, criminal activity among the drug community and prison.

As you would imagine, work in a community like ours brings us into close contact with all kinds of social issues; parental drug & alcohol abuse, chronic debt, abuse, bereavement, sickness, crime – the list goes on. Although we started out as a youth project we were not able to hold on to that identity for very long, we soon became aware that young people's families, however broken and messed up, are a really crucial part of their life. They are often the cause of a young person's problems, they are sometimes the solution and commonly both.

One of the greatest assets to our youth work has been the development, in recent years, of our Family Support project. Our family support worker Nicci works as an integral part of the Eden team but with the specific intention of working with children under ten years old and their parents. So she runs toddler groups, a kids club and a baby church as well as parenting classes and all kinds of other training for parents; she also spends a good amount of time visiting families at home. Often these are homes where our teenagers live, and while Nicci is providing a great support to parents and smaller children, other team members are mentoring the teenagers . The overall effect of working with a whole family is significant. If we work through issues with a teenager in isolation and then return them to their family it is likely that any progress that the young person has made will quickly be undone as there is little or no understanding of the journey which has taken place. Engaging a whole family in the development is slower and more costly but is more likely to result in lasting transformation.

This whole family approach is particularly powerful and the Church may well be the best organisation to deliver such services. Whereas other services are often limited by their professional agenda such as health, education, under 5s, 13-19s etc we are able to offer a joined up service where we offer support to people of all ages and circumstances. That is not to say that the professional services are of no value. Their work is vital, but often it needs somebody to provide a consistent point of focus in an extremely chaotic environment. Our role here is to become advocates for the whole family, helping them to find stability, and where there are chronic issues such as addiction or debt, helping them to access the best services which are available to them.

Would it be beneficial and possible to move your work towards a "whole family approach"?

Some years ago our church were praying together and we felt God was drawing us to Isaiah 62, which is a chapter about the rebuilding of the city of Jerusalem. As we studied these verses in depth together we discovered many great promises that we still hang onto believing that the redemptive process described could be true not only of the great city of Jerusalem but also for a little estate in Manchester.

> *'No longer will they call you Deserted or your name Desolate. But you will be called Hephzibah and your land Beulah; for the lord will take delight in you and your land will be married' (Isaiah 62:4)*

The whole chapter has a sense about it that the old has gone and a new day is coming, that the time is coming when God will make the land beautiful and fruitful again and that the crop which our land produces will be ours to enjoy – not plundered by the enemy. Our prayer is that this fruit is our children, our young people, who will find fulfilment and discover potential in their lives and as they reach that potential will find themselves restored in their relationships with one another, with their families, with creation and with God.

It might seem like a pipe dream but on 5th September 2005 The Royal Bank of Scotland listed Openshaw as the second most desirable place in England to buy a house: quite ironic considering we are still in the top 1% of most deprived communities in Britain. Perhaps they had read Isaiah 62 as well!

Perhaps it goes without saying that for all the joys of the work we've been doing in Openshaw there have been many, many sorrows – sorrows of disappointment when a young person doesn't come through. Or worse, when they do come through, even to faith. and then they fall away and don't want to know us, when the addict goes back to their old life after months of being clean or dry, when a young person just won't engage in the mentoring program and they can't see their life potential slipping away.

At times like these you inevitably reflect on yourself and on the things you did and said or didn't do and didn't say. You quickly come to the realisation that yes, you could have done much, much more to prevent this but that it is all part of the struggle, the cross we bear. There is a weariness that can come if we are not ever so careful. We become less affected by the condition of our young people, by their tragic circumstances and by their disadvantage. The media call it 'compassion fatigue' which is a posh name for 'we're tired of caring'. I need to be constantly on my guard against this.

Youth work in a poor urban setting like ours is very different to anything that I had experienced in the suburbs, and it has changed me in so many ways. The needs are many and varied and whilst I have offered a few examples of programs in this chapter I cannot account for all the incidental interventions which have occurred between team members and young people on the streets of Openshaw, in the paper shop or in the park, which have probably had at least equal bearing on the how the work has unfolded. Much has been done, some of which has been powerful and effective, and much of which we can only say are learning experiences of 'how not to' engage in urban youth work.

How have the past few months or years of youth work and ministry changed you?

As with all types of ministry, sometimes the task can just seem so huge you don't know where to begin, but in our experience doing something small has always led us onto something else. It has been something like a box of tissues – as you pull one out the next one follows.

The vision for our church has always been to see our community transformed from the broken, fragmented ruin that it has become to a vibrant community full of life and fruit. My personal belief is that amidst all the debris, God's kingdom is already here sown into the fabric of the land and into the lives of our neighbours and friends, and our job is simply to point out, uncover and explain the wonder of God as he appears all around us.

For further reflection ...

Gary Bishop speaks at the beginning of his article about a "sense of calling" and "vocation"; there is a strong sense that it was this that sustained him and the team through some difficult transitions and some painful experiences.

Do you think that a calling and vocation is an important ingredient for work with young people?

Are there experiences, events or, perhaps, biblical verses that you identify with your sense of calling and that you can look back upon for encouragement when times are hard?

CHAPTER THREE

A Church for the Unchurched

St. Lawrence's, Reading

Chris Russell

This chapter is about our experiences at St. Lawrence parish church in Reading. Although we are one of many parish churches in the city centre, we are almost the parish church for young people in Reading – we have a mandate and vocation to work amongst non churched young people, see them come to faith and build new forms of church with them. Nearly all our growth has come from young people who have had no previous contact with church and what I want to focus on here is what has been the hardest aspect of our ministry – how to build a discipling community at the heart of the church. Yet, it is this vision and the struggle to make progress towards it that has made us more committed and convinced of our vocation as a church for young people. But, what does being such a church mean in practice?

My sense is that the hundreds of people who give time to investing in young people know frustration, challenge but above all a deep sense of the significance of what we are called to do. This is true of all aspects of youth ministry. Whilst there has been much made in the past of the difference in youth ministry between those in church based work and those in projects with those who are non churched, it is essential that the significance and place of church based work isn't for a moment decried. So whilst it is a truism to say that much church based youth work has focused on those who are already in the faith, in nurturing and developing this faith, there should be no grounds for not giving those involved in this ministry full respect.

However, there are those of us who can't quite comprehend what it must be like to have a group of teenagers sit through and take part in one of those ready made sessions in Youthwork magazines, and even more incomprehensible is the idea that they might sit and listen to a four minute song, then discuss the significance of the lyrics to their lives. The chasm between churched and non churched young people seems to be yawning wider by the year. The measurements of this yawn are not our concern in this chapter; rather, I want to just set out how one small initiative in Reading is seeking to be both a mission community to young people who have not conceived of considering faith and a community which takes commitment and growth in faith seriously.

Do you also see this chasm opening up where you live and work?

St. Laurence Reading is first and foremost a collective of people around a mission. And for me, the place of local church in mission amongst young people is a given. Of course there are many great para-church organisations who empower, envision and resource working with young people. There are fantastic initiatives which are made possible by huge sacrifice, commitment and expertise. But without any apology I will always bang the drum loudly and uncompromisingly (though not terribly rhythmically) for local church being God's best instrument of mission. I know I need to get to the stories, but briefly here's why…

The other year I heard a famous Christian on a stage tell young people they had to go back to their homes and schools and 'be Jesus to people'. This was because they were Christians and, apparently, 'Christian' meant 'little Christ'. Now, it might just be that I haven't read the right bit of church history, but I am baffled where that definition of Christian comes from. Cos I can't find it anywhere! Christian means those who are followers of Christ. But as for 'being Jesus to people' – it's a task which he is more than able to do, as he is alive and willing. But not just that; how on earth is a young person supposed to bear the burden of being Jesus? Most of them find it hard enough to be themselves! And does this not encourage saviour complexes?

But the church, the body of Christ – that the community that are called to be Jesus to people. So it's not an individual thing, it's a corporate thing. Therefore, those of us who passionately believe Jesus Christ is the one whose questions, claims, love, life, words, character, wisdom, sacrifice, forgiveness, presence, and hope are the transformative realities of this world, have to take with the utmost seriousness the place of his body here on earth in the transformation of lives.

So, when we began some 6 years ago, we wondered how we were going to begin to fulfil this mandate to be a church living to see young people come to faith and build new models of church with them. Me, I had ideas of becoming a local celeb on the schools circuit, doing lessons, assemblies etc. This was swiftly burst by a member of the small community of 10 who were committed to the vision; no, that would just make me feel good, and wouldn't allow for healthy relationships to be built with the whole community.

Have you felt the temptation to base your work around what makes you look and feel good? Are there trusted people around to help you resist this temptation?

So we decided: ours wasn't the vocation of Christian education; ours was about being a community, to which relationship would be all important. We decided to pray and see what opened up; to wait for the gold seam, then mine it. This sounds simplistic, but it contains this radical notion that we aren't just bringing God into a situation, a place, a group of people from which he has been absent; instead, we are asking him to open up our eyes to see what he has been up to, what he has been uncovering, what he has been making possible, and what he intends to do.

So when the gold seam opened up we invested in it. It was a local school where we were soon around two days a week meeting young people referred to us by heads of year because of 'behavioural' issues, which were rooted in so much more than being bored by Wilfred Owen's war poems. On the back of this we kept praying, and we wondered what the next step might be for getting the gold out.

Rather than learn how to skateboard, or pop along to Quiksilver and buy some new clothes, our sense was that authentic mission was done by people being themselves. Therefore we wondered whether if we just intentionally did the things that we enjoyed doing and invited young people to be part of them we might be able to grow these relationships. So we started a pool club, a cinema club and a dance club. These became great places to nurture the contacts we had first met through schools work.

But whilst it was great to be able to introduce these young people to the wider community at these events, there was a distinct lack of them asking us for a reason for the hope we had within us. It was time to be intentional again, and through various hits and misses, we welcomed a couple of handfuls of young people into the church building to explore the mysteries of God's love, in the form of a carol service which they led and an Easter 'labyrinth' in which they helped put together an experiential journey of the cross.

The Easter labyrinth was really a hotchpotch affair. Behind it was the desire to give young people who we had begun investing in relationally an opportunity to explore the seismic events of holy week. We knew it wasn't about us putting something on and inviting them to it, they needed more buy – in than that. And we sensed that the process of putting it together would be as important as the 'event' itself. On top of this we were convinced that the events of holy week and Easter spoke for themselves, that the story engaged any who entered it, and so we didn't want to give information about these events, but wanted young people to explore them for themselves and begin to experience them.

So, just after the school carol service we put it to a dozen young people, who hadn't ever stepped into a church building until that Christmas, that we needed them to help us put together something for Easter. And so in the weeks leading up to Easter we sat round chewing the story and asking them how we could invite people into it. They came up with an idea about how Jesus was treated leads us to ask questions of ourselves, and so they wanted to use lots of mirrors with bits of the story on, reflecting our true selves back to us, bits we didn't want to see. There was a love-themed room, which contrasted fluffy romance with bloody nails. There were the obligatory candles, a huge cross on which you had to write an inscription to put above his head, and a dark dead-end tunnel. It was a health and safety nightmare – all those drapes and ladders and ropes and projector leads. It wasn't radically creative or world shatteringly unique: in fact, you could probably do better. But it was theirs. And so they loved it, they grasped it, and it grasped them. Their mates came and they showed them round, and I think even one of their parents showed up. That was a very good Friday.

Once you have started to open the door on the drama of God and invite young people in, the joy is in seeing it take in lives. This is a journey we are still on, one of stops and starts, sprints and times of cramp. The community continues to be orientated around those who aren't part of us. But this community isn't apart to these young people. It's essential to their contact and development. Having a community at the heart of what we invite young people to be part of means that what they are presented with is more than some cognitive facts to assent to, or an ethical code to apply to their individual lives, but a group of people where Jesus is known, celebrated and loved and a community in which he reshapes our lives.

At this precise moment do you feel that your ministry is in a time of stopping/cramping or of starting/sprinting? How can you make the most of the time you are in?

So for us this collective is vital to the invitation. It's not that church is a secondary activity that a young person needs to get their head round after they have got their head round the personal stuff, it's primary.

The other year I met this really impressive guy. You could tell he was impressive cos he had lots of figures, lots of proof of the impact he had. Proof of how many young people his organization saw each week, how many assemblies were done, how many lessons were taught and how many individuals heard the good news through this ministry. So I just asked" "What happens to them next?"

Apparently you just have to hope they get picked up by a local church.

But what if it's a local church that meets them in their world that engages with them, and doesn't just try to mirror their world or somehow make Jesus relevant to their world? Is it just me that finds such language toe curling? It's the same idea that goes in the song where we kindly offer God our insight that we live to make him famous. No Jesus has just got to be introduced to people in order for him to start to engage with their world. Our challenge is that we relay the authentic Jesus. And my sense is that, as he is at work already in his world, he will engage and interact with each young person in particular ways, in specifics rather than generalities.

In all this being a church which had a mandate to 'do things differently' we had a license to push what worship looked like; how people engaged in the things of God. And this we did with relative verve. As convinced charismatics, the non-negotiable was the presence of the present God, in praise, word, sacraments, prayer, healing, and life-sharing. We had found it relatively easy to find ways to offering young people connection with God. But it wasn't a spirituality which was transformative. It didn't ask anything beyond the event itself. And whilst it was always moving to pray about granny and just-been-born nephews, it became clear that what these guys needed wasn't some spiritual service provider, just there to distribute a sense of God when that was necessary. What wasn't needed was a shot of God into a God shaped hole. What was needed was God shaped lives.

So discipleship became and has remained a major preoccupation. Mostly in the fact that we haven't got to the top of the hill yet. We remain insistent that lives for God are lives which look radically different and transformed. The question is the 'how then shall we live?'. And whilst my reflexes tell me I know the answers to that one, I have always found Bishop Graham Cray's adage about his own ideas and his teenagers daughter's discipleship helpful, when he says "I realise that my experience and insight was about as much good as King Saul's armour to the shepherd boy David as he went to fight Goliath". And he goes on to throw the challenge down as to whether we fully trust that God's Spirit can forge, white hot lives amongst teens in this generation. The fact that we might not know exactly what such a life will look like is not the issue. That we should strive to not accept anything less than such lives is.

So I will always remember a conversation with a key young member of the church, two weeks before she was due to be baptised. "Now Chris, are you saying if I get baptised I must never sleep with anyone again till I get married?" Because I am sure you will have an opinion on that one, I won't let on what I said. But how does discipleship fit in here? If you say 'yes' is it really grace? Do you ask each person to be baptised only if they will commit not to gossip again? Does *not* being part of the family of faith enable such changes to happen? And if you say 'no' – is that just cheap grace?

Our experience is that it is in this community that God grows disciples; as lives are shared and grace, obedience, questions, expectations are the frame for living. And the old often tripped out statement of 'belong, believe, behave'? Yes of course. But if you're really part of such a community you will have tears in your eyes for the pain that you go through in waiting, investing and praying for discipleship in others' lives. As Paul says 'I am in the pangs of childbirth till Christ is fully formed in you." (Gal 4: 19.)

Is this pain a part of your experience of working with young people? What do you think is God's purpose in our feeling this pain?

But our experience is also the 'how then shall we live?' question. The flavour of a God shaped life isn't just a course for those who have made the Christian faith their own. Discussions which seek to discern and forge out lives shaped around and for God are conversations which invite many in. I will always remember that my attempt to do a Christian basics course at St. Laurence based around the key doctrines of the faith only took off when we happened to go off on a tangent about forgiveness and a girl threw down her bible and stormed out of the building, shouting no one was going to tell her she had to forgive her dad. From that moment on we covered issues like truth telling, your body, family, love, and pleasure. Its not that we got it right; it's that I got it wrong in thinking the way these guys were going to engage in the things of God was creed-ally, not life-fully.

So the decision not to settle for anything less than God shaped lives was a vital one for us. Otherwise we could have just gone for big experiences, for creative ways of trying to get young people to engage with God. Our experience was that our young people loved lighting candles to ambient dance music for sick relatives, loved dropping stones in buckets and tasting honey comb. However, if that was all we were doing, we had just become a spiritual service provider. And whilst it was at times a fruitful way to begin a journey of faith, it was no way to see it continued.

To really commit to this means understanding that young people are not clients. They are not those we do things for or to. They are those we climb with. That spare room in my house can't remain empty when a 16 year old girl has had to move out of her house because her step father has been physically abusive to her, or if that year 10 boy who is on his last warning if he bunks school again needs someone to wake him up and make sure he gets to school for two weeks running. These young people made in God's image must be let into our lives, because the only way a life gets shaped into the shape of Jesus' is by being shared with his church. If you are simply seeing young people once a week at a worship event which they just come to, nothing much is going to shift. We have found the weight of what they are part of in the family of God needs to be heavier than anything else they are part of. And there can be no soft focus on the sacrifice that this requires.

So, members of the church have painted rooms, put off holidays, stayed up all night, wept, cooked, accompanied to court, moved furniture, been kept on hold by social services for 45 minutes; gone to solicitors, education welfare meetings at school, pre-natal scans, post-abortion counselling; sat on pavements of Reading outside pubs, and joined the mourners at funerals. And we should have done much more! There are no quick fixes or solutions. The gospel takes ages to really truly take in lives. But is there anything like the privilege of seeing it unfurl?

We constantly remind ourselves: our young people are made for him. Their lives are best when God has got hold of them, when they are lived towards him, at full pelt, with nothing held back.

So this summer we are involved in a town wide mission. Each church in Reading has been urged to embark on a new initiative in mission. We are doing a Noise project: 50 teenagers involved in making a difference to the town. At least half of them wouldn't call themselves Christians. But they know we are, and they know they want to be involved in doing things for others. Already they are getting the bug. It's like there's something in the water during these kind of weeks, as people realise how good it is do things for others, how good it is to love.

But why does that surprise me? My theology of humanity is rooted in Genesis 1 rather than Genesis 3. The other day we got a leaflet through the door from a local church which had this opening gambit; 'God's verdict on all people is the same; everyone stands under his judgement and deserves to be sent to hell.' Despite there being a bit in me which respects their hard nosed attitude which obviously cares little for anything further on the leaflet being read, this is an outrage. Surely our first word on humanity should be; 'God's verdict on everyone is the same; we are made in his image and for his glory, we are the objects of his love and salvation, and when we live in relationship with him we discover who we are made to be.'

What is your "default setting"? Do you naturally see young people as fallen sinners or as made in the image of God?

But I refuse to believe that exclusion, smoking pot, casual sex, criminal records, disengagement, hot temper, and disrespect is what any of the young people in God's world were made for. This stuff isn't natural to them. Yes, it might have become second nature to them. But first nature – those are the things of God. Each person is made for God, flourishes in light and only finds fulfilment in God's ways for them. So when we offer people these chances to explore being part of God's actions in doing things for others, or in framing their lives around God's ways, we find that this good news is the best news for them, and that God's image in them shines when they reflect his ways.

For further reflection ...

Chris Russell speaks a great deal of authenticity – authentic Christians, the authentic Christ, authentic community, authentic discipleship. The trouble is that authenticity cannot be captured, packaged or duplicated; we each have to work out for ourselves what authenticity looks like for us in our context. We can start by asking:

When I am with young people do I present the real me or a carefully constructed image of the ideal youth worker?

When I dream of a young person developing as a person and growing in Christ do I imagine them turning into a "mini-me" or finding their own Christlikeness?

Am I working towards a community that resembles my idea of the perfect church or am I willing to let God call something fresh into existence?

CHAPTER FOUR

A Hub of Hope

Church.co.uk, London

Pete Brierley

In October 2003 I started painting my new office at Christ Church and Upton Chapel (soon to become church.co.uk) in Waterloo, just north of Brixton and just south of Big Ben. I didn't know then that I was to be a youth worker; rather I had hoped I would be a 'real' pastor.

Did you choose youthwork or fall into it? Do you now see it as a stepping stone or as a long-term commitment?

Steve Chalke had a dream to turn a dormant church in Central London into a hive of activity. It was my job, with a team of others, to help this church of 15 elderly men and women grow into being the heartbeat of the community. I soon discovered the heartbeat and doorway to any community are the children and young people, but with none available where could I start? Pete Ward once wrote, for every five pieces of church based youth work you do, you should aim to do at least one piece of community youth work; for church.co.uk the next 3 years were a reversal of this. Every Friday night, with a football at my feet, a good friend, Matt Williams, by my side and a vision to see God's Kingdom grow, I took to the local cages, challenging local young people to a 5 a-side.

Young people would ask me what my job was and I would tell

them with pride, "it's my job to make sure you lot are doing okay". Friday nights grew into a regular feature of our week; we would play football, stop fights, encourage unity and ensure local young people had fun. In 4 years we've gone from a random programme of detached youth work to having our own youth centre, a community radio station, starting a football league, a mentoring programme and face to face work with over 100 young people a week. Many of the young people we work with are not always friendly or easy to help they live chaotic lives, carry knives, have dropped out of school and have had to win respect by fighting their way to the top of the teenage food chain. They all have one thing in common: they are made in the image of God and have masses of potential.

Since the early days, much has happened to get to where we are now. There are many stories to tell and many scars recording them. How have we done it? Mainly blood, sweat, prayer and tears, and then some more.

From nothing to something

Ricky, Freddy, and Charlie lived on the estate behind the church. I'd never met them but they soon became essential to the development of our youth work. Harriet was Freddy's twin sister and on 17th April 2002 she unexpectedly died, forcing us as a church community to respond. At 23 years old the prospect of visiting a family who had just lost a 12 year old girl was nerve racking. I didn't have the pastoral experience to help an elderly person with gout, let alone this. You'll find this happens a lot to youth workers; you're thrown in the deep end and expected to swim!! Terrified, I went round and met the boys; and went with them to the funeral. Ricky, who was 16 when I met him, became the backbone of our early youth work and the inspiration for much that went on at church.co.uk. Harriet's tragic death forced us to open our doors, our lives and our hearts to local issues and local youths. The Hub was born, a Thursday night youth club. It was nothing special… in fact it was nothing more than an extended hand and a listening ear. Youth work should always start with listening, sometimes for years. On the first night it was just Ricky, his 2 brothers and an old table tennis table that I found from years gone by.

Sometimes the most tragic events have the most positive consequences; have you seen this in your work?

Listening soon turned into action and we began to respond to local need as required. Responding to local need is at the core of who we are as a church. John tells us "the word became flesh and dwelt among us"[1]. We must dwell in our communities and through our living we must bring about God's Kingdom, his shalom, that fullness of life to all that we meet, whether Muslim or Jew, male or female, rich or poor, young or old.

As more young people started coming to our poor excuse for a youth club we continued to respond to some of the problems that some of these young people so clearly had. One of the first things we started to do was mentor young people at risk of exclusion from school. I promised to help Robert with his Religious Education G.C.S.E if he promised to teach me to rap. If I'm honest, neither of us had much success but it brought me closer to another young person and made me realise just how fragile these young peoples lives are. Robert was in a dead-end school; he had a father who beat him, a mother who had disowned him and a dog that would bite your arm off. He was in a gang with other young people, all of whom had similar issues and caused a lot of trouble in South London during the first summer I was there. Violence ruled our streets. We decided it was our responsibility as the church to get involved and so, having spoken with local council and other youth organisations, we came up with the idea of running a local radio station. Southside FM was born and in just 4 weeks 600 young people had got involved. The importance of positive activities for young people is often underestimated. After a 12 yr old boy was shot dead in Liverpool recently, in an inspirational cry of desperation, British rapper Dizzee Rascal asked young people to divert whatever energy they put into gang violence, robbery, and antisocial behaviour into whatever it was they loved to do; singing, rapping, dancing, acting, football, even ballet. The trouble is there isn't always the opportunity to pursue something you love. Southside became this outlet; it was a magnet attracting some of the most talented people I've ever met in my life to a radio studio in our church. We've had hip hop artists, lovers of rock, singers and even had whole crews come down and perform together.

Police commented that street crime had hit an all time low. (Perhaps because most of it was taking place in our church.) Southside was the start of our church's response to low self-esteem in young people, local gang crime, low employment and lack of positive role models.

It's amazing looking back and seeing how things have so radically and organically developed. Southside now has its own studio and media suite and is an online radio station (www.southsideradio.co.uk) running throughout the year, diverting young people from crime, giving them an opportunity to express their opinions, showcase their talent and learn new skills.

Last year, a fellow youth worker and friend Tim Broadbent took our Friday night football to the next level, by forming a local estates football league and 3 teams; an under 10s under 12s and 16+. Tim and a group of volunteers are currently coaching the older young people, who have just started to play in a local league. They've just secured funding to get their own kit with a badge that will say 'hub athletic'. Tim's turned football from a Friday night social into an activity that encourages unity andcommunity cohesion, tackles racism andgang warfare, increases healthy living and boosts self-esteem. In short, football, just like Southside FM, sees to it that the Kingdom of God grows in this place.

In this account football and radio flourished; what might inspire and motivate the young people you work with?

But where's the conversion and what has Jesus got to do with football and radio stations? Jesus met people where they were at and took them on a journey to experience shalom – fullness of life. Young people need to be met where they are at, whether that is a football pitch, a local cage or a coffee bar. Some of the young people have started coming to our more formal expression of church on a Sunday morning, some have started asking their own questions of faith. They sometimes pray before games, and they have all experienced God's grace and welcome from our community. People from our congregation go and watch the lads play their matches on a Saturday morning and we consider them to be as much a part of our community as anyone else. They're learning the radical message of Jesus without all the cultural packaging.

For example, recently young people came up with the concept of showing their experience of life through photos, in an exhibition entitled "A day in the life of a young person". Photos ranged from pictures of police cars to a picture of a crucifix, each photo full of insight and meaning, describing the lives of urban young people in a really interesting way. The winning image was photographed by a Muslim boy, Mohammed, who has been a part of our church for 4 years now. He had taken a picture of a piece of graffiti that simply said "Change your life". Mohammed's brother had recently been in trouble with the police for robbery and GBH, and I had sat with the family who spoke of their dismay at what could be done and their fear that Mohammed was changing and might also get sucked into this life of chaotic crime. Later the same day I saw Mohammed's photo echoing Jesus' sentiments and the apostle Paul's words to become a new creation, and marvelled that once again the message of Christ had somehow found its way through a mass of cultural barriers to the heart of a 16 yr old Muslim boy.

"Therefore, if anyone is in Christ, he is a new creation; the old has gone, the new has come!" (2 Corinthians 5:17)

A vision for young people

I have come to realise that church can take on lots of different shapes and sizes. People tell me the church is dying in this country. I keep hearing it. The truth is, the church is flourishing, but we're only looking to the graveyard for signs of life. Traditional church for many people doesn't help them connect with God anymore, however they do connect with God and others in different ways. Why is it so strange to us that our hip-hop loving young people are leaving our churches that sing soft rock? Why do we think all young people will connect with wooden pews, old pulpits and ancient hymns? As long as we keep bashing out the same chords and the same sermons we're missing out on connecting with God in new and real ways.

God is throwing a feast and inviting people to the party but we're too busy with church to notice. Instead he's started to invite the gangsters, those with antisocial behaviour. He's gone way beyond the boundaries of church and he's choosing to build his kingdom with those we consider to be the least. I believe that every one of the young people we work with experiences God in some small way and I believe that every one of them worships him whether it's in the songs they sing, the dances they choreograph or the football they play. They may not know it, but they're sat at the table eating the feast and sooner or later they're gonna wake up and ask: "Who's the host?"[2]

I went to a lecture that Pete Ward delivered about his book *Liquid Church* Pete was encouraging us to grow church outside the boundaries of what we traditionally consider to be church. Rather than our rituals it is the relationships that we have that unite us, our connection with Christ and with one another. But how does a liquid church escape the dilemma of evaporating or running down drains without anyone realising? In other words, how does what we do at church.co.uk with local young people connect with other aspects of the church? Someone stood up in the seminar and came up with what I feel is a rather good picture of how the church should be liquid on the outside and solid in the middle.

We have a strong core of people who are a part of our community. They love God, are passionate about his word and passionately pursue the Kingdom of God. Without this solid core driving our vision and moulding our ethos we wouldn't be able to do youth work that reaches beyond what others see as a border. We create as many opportunities for this core to meet with other, more liquid, parts of our church. We encourage our senior minister Dave to come and support the young people who are in the local football team. He cheers them on in their endeavours to be great at football but also in their pursuit for meaningful community and search for a God that makes sense of their troubled lives.

I recently went to Washington DC. If I'm honest I went kicking and screaming: seeing the White House and memorials of dead presidents didn't seem like my idea of fun. What I found was truly inspirational: a city that is beautiful and so well designed. To the less observant tourist, Washington is designed rather randomly, but to the keener eye you note that it's all connected. If you stand at Lincoln's memorial, you can see Washington's Memorial and Capitol Hill; if you stand off centre at Jefferson's memorial you can see Lincoln's memorial; from Roosevelt's you can see Washington's and... well, you get the idea. Each memorial is linked to another, threading the spirit of Washington weblike across the whole city. Similarly, our youth work is designed that from one activity you have the opportunity to view, and then hopefully participate in, other parts of our community.

It's connections that make what we do so special connections between local young people who play football and our Sunday morning congregation, connections between parents of children and staff who work in our coffee shop. In this way life spreads, the vision of our church gets shared, people's lives get transformed, and church happens accidentally on the way.

Are there potential links and connections to bring young people from "outside" into contact with committed Christians in your local community?

To be honest

Of course the flip side of vision is frustration. I get frustrated by the lack of resources, frustrated by being so understaffed, frustrated with myself for not being able to do a better job, raise more funds, be harder working or change more lives. My frustration should lead me to my knees and cause me to rely on God, the author and perfecter not just of our faith but our visions too. Sadly, I end up working late nights, neglecting my wife and wearing myself out.

There are times when I wish I didn't do my job I sometimes feel sick with fear before I run events or before a session. Why? Because the young people I work with aren't middle class, middle of the road, sit down and listen to a Bible story type kids. They're the type of kids that use snooker cues for weapons. In fact, we started trying to hide equipment on Thursday nights after there had been a few incidents in which Frisbees had been used as weapons. After a couple of weeks we realised that we'd soon have nothing left, as even pool balls had been put into a sock and swung round menacingly. Just up the road a fight broke out amongst young people who'd taken hockey sticks and were using them to batter members of an opposing gang; it resulted in the death of a 15-year-old church going boy.

I've been threatened with knives, I've had a young person try and head butt me, I've found myself in the middle of gang war zones, or holding onto a fighting dog trying to stop it from biting me. Youth work is not and should not be an easy ride, a permanent state of euphoric glee; it's painful, and difficult. As I always say to members of our community: "There's no handle on the cross"[3]. It's not a lunch box that you can swing up and down whilst whistling the latest Matt Redman chorus. You carry it on your back; it wounds you, scarring you for life. It means you have things stolen from your church, it means you can't preach pretty sermons, have glib answers or have uninterrupted worship; in short it means that life is more difficult, more painful but more real and certainly more rewarding.

What do you find most challenging about your work ... is it danger or boredom that you struggle with?

When I first started at church.co.uk in October 2003 – just after I'd finished painting that wall I told you about – I sat in a room with my new boss. Steve is quite a character, a force to be reckoned with, passionate, visionary and wise. I remember feeling young and fresh with my whole life ahead of me. Steve looked at me and said "you think you're young, don't you… but in 10 years time you'll be 32 and you'll wonder: "Where did the last 10 years of my life go?". These words have haunted me and inspired me to suck every ounce out of life, and to get on doing the stuff of life that really matters most. I have a vision to see young people experience something of God's love and grace through music, radio, sports, dance and good relationships, and I intend to see this vision through.

Whatever you are doing and wherever you are doing it, may God bless you as you reach beyond the boundaries of conventional church, and as you do you may remember the apostle Paul's words:

> *"We are hard pressed on every side, but not crushed; perplexed, but not in despair; persecuted, but not abandoned; struck down, but not destroyed. We always*

carry around in our body the death of Jesus, so that the life of Jesus may also be revealed in our body,"[4]

Notes

1 John Chapter 1:1
2 The parable of the Great Banquet Luke 14:15-24
3 Kosuke Koyama "No handle on the Cross"
4 2 Corinthians 4:8-10

For further reflection ...

Pete Brierley says, "The flip side of vision is frustration ... My frustration should lead me to my knees and cause me to rely on God, the author and perfecter not just of our faith but our visions too."

What frustrates you most about the work you are doing with young people?

If you "flip" this over, might it be possible to prayerfully interpret and channel this frustration into a renewed and more perfect vision for ministry?

What would be different about your ministry if you envisioned a way of dealing with your greatest frustrations?

CHAPTER FIVE

Connecting Church Youth Ministry to the Community

St. Paul's, Hammersmith

Lucy Hawes

London's full of contrasts, especially in urban youth subcultures. In a typical London borough you're guaranteed to see skaters hanging around in concrete clans, sixth former students filling parks and coffee shops, street gangs staking their territorial claims or church kids flitting in and out of Christianity. Universally each substratum of youth culture takes on a different form of expression and flaunts its unique identity by where it hangs out, the street chic it sports and the vernacular it uses. The not-new question is how do youth workers and the church reach these disparate groups with the gospel from the outpost of the local church?

St. Paul's, Hammersmith

St. Paul's church's mission statement is to be 'a transforming community for Hammersmith and beyond' and it aims to fulfil this by enabling the church to be the church, which doesn't mean one youth worker doing all the youth work. Instead it means challenging church members, whatever their skills and background, to get into urban mission. As well as a full-time youth church we have embarked on a road to doing mission through the setting up of a designated youth charity, W6 Youthworks, whose aim is to provide services for local young people. Starting up this charity is an attempt to let the church be the church, but at the same time to enable the church to be a resource to the local community. This arrangement means that we can access all the skills of church without straining church structures too much, as the charity is independently financed and therefore we can still invest in the youth church and promote the two simultaneously in the local area.

St Paul's have chosen to create a "youth church". Do you agree that sometimes this is a good way forward? Why or why not?

Another part of this mission statement is to encourage the church to be the church to each other, which can be translated into encouraging the youth church to do mission to the local neighbourhood and their friends by becoming a youth church which exists in and of themselves and incorporates their way of worshipping God. The aim of this is to have young people being church for their friends and for the local community unfettered by the main church. We are in a fortunate position to be employing a full time youth worker to oversee this but, slogans and strap lines aside, we realise that while it is the task of the whole church to reach into the lives of young people, youth culture often is somewhat removed from the mainstream congregation and its Sunday services which is why we do have very specific and targeted youth work, albeit under the spiritual canopy of the church.

Inner city issues

The issues of youth culture in Hammersmith are replicated all over the capital and many parts of the country. A young man was stabbed to death streets away from our church; single parent families are the norm; drug and alcohol binges are frequent; and young offenders repeatedly end up re-offending. Meanwhile, gun crime and gang culture seem never to be out of the headlines. This phenomenon outside the church is only half the story for youth ministers. In my experience, young people claiming to be Christians are addicted to internet porn, think that no sex before marriage is an archaic principle and/or believe that you can be a Buddhist and a Christian. So the challenges and the channels of communication may look different for churched and unchurched youth, but the need for mission and discipleship to each young person remains the same. In many ways the divisions we as a church have made are unrepresentative of reality.

What are the biggest temptations that Christian young people struggle with where you work?

The charity option

W6 youthworks follows a model of inter-dependency already established between St. Paul's and another satellite charity associated with the church called Spear. Spear runs a hugely successful programme for unemployed 16-24 year-olds, providing them with career, life and marketing skills. Spear's phenomenal success rate has been picked up by the Conservative party as a shining example of social entrepreneurs in the voluntary sector doing a better job than the public sector. Based on similar foundations, W6 youthworks is reviewing all the social issues affecting young people in the area and coming up with schemes to tackle these problems. Various ideas are in the pipeline, from bike mechanic courses, homework clubs and teaching pupils in years 7 and 9 about the unwritten rules at school. Paramount to the success of the W6 initiative is not only the funding and the partnership with from local bodies, including the church, but also the existing relationships with young people in the area that have been developed over the years through the church-run Friday night youth group, the Bridge. By having a club in place already, access to funding and support is made easier as there is already an area of known need for youth provision. Other starting blocks for W6 have been the church's annual week of mission, Kiss the Street week, which provides an opportunity for a week long youth café at the beginning of the summer holidays and an event called the Vibe. The Vibe attracts around 150 young people and parents by showcasing young urban talent from the local area and then adds a big dollop of the gospel by inviting Christian artists to perform and be involved in the event. This year the success of the Regenerate youth bus also bolstered numbers at the café even without all the usual workshops and activities being put on.

The church option

Meanwhile the young people already part of the church have a weekly group equivalent to a youth church and a host of usual church activity provision. The difference is that these young people are being peppered with opportunities for local mission. While the two aspects of the church's youth work act independently at some points, the overall aim is integration, whereby the churched young people, already largely from the local area, become a church welcoming and reaching out in a suitable and authentic way to the lives of other young people in the neighbourhood. We see that, regardless of spiritual proximity to the church, the message of new beginnings and real life in Christ is the same for all young people, and the pressures, difficulties and temptations in and out of the church are still the same. One way we have nurtured the churched youth into an outward, missional perspective is through inviting them to be part of the church's mission week. Young people relish participation and more than that, they see God at work, they meet and are challenged by Christians and non-Christians; they are part of the kingdom.

To further integrate our areas of work we have devised a teaching and a practical mission week for our church kids as a week of mission at home. The benefits of this are that they remain part of the community and so the relationships they make can last; we can partner with other churches and invite their young people to join us and so build up a body of young believers in the area; these young people support one another during the week and become further integrated into the whole church body. In the coming year we will build on the success of an alternative worship event we held in the middle of this mission week that exemplifies how we want youth church to grow. Young people, both Christian and non-Christian, both from our church and other churches, and of all different nationalities, came together and we saw a glimpse of young people worshipping together, almost in their own tongues, despite background, appearance and attitude.

Are you able to offer young people opportunities not just to receive but to go and to give?

Alternative worship for all

The worship event came on the back of previous failed worship events. We had been considering for some time how to bridge the gap between the work we do with the church kids and the different dynamic with the unchurched youth and so had done music events to appeal to both but not really achieved a successful crossover. Yet here there seemed to be the potential scenario for unorthodox yet curiously-orthodox church, right in our midst, right at the heart of our urban youth ministry. The background will help crystallise the scenario; historically the needs of the churched young people and the unchurched young people have been served very differently. The church-going group meet on a Sunday morning for worship and have teaching with small groups for the 11-13s and 14-18s during the week. There are also camps during the holidays and socials haphazardly throughout the year. Perhaps atypically for a middle class London church the youth work has grown out of an ever-expanding children's work. Like many youth groups the core churched young people are from churched families and there is a sense that they have grown up together and are sometimes there as much socially as spiritually. The aim of the mid-week groups is to engender relational and spiritual belonging for the young people at different and distinct stages in their physical and spiritual growth. The unchurched young people have a regular Friday night youth group, summer camps and occasional workhops, socials and, of course, the Vibe.

The beauty of this event was that it had elements familiar to both groups and it also mixed in a third element. The two groups use shared facilities, so both felt comfortable; the youth worship band played Christian songs, and an older youth from the Vibe committee and the Friday night group gave a testimony. But as a third factor there were also new people there which made no-one feel new and everyone feel new. The event, like any ambitious youth worship evening, was a bit chaotic, filled with prayer but structured to make things move quickly so no-one got bored and everyone felt included. The young people who had come to the café for the week or who were helping out as part of the mission week provided a sedative to some of the rowdier bunch who weren't Christians but were part of the W6 Kiss the Street week. We advertised it to the core of the local youth but not on a mass scale, preferring word of mouth rather than mass hype, we recruited from the church stable and we encouraged key leaders to bring friends.

Are there unconventional forms of advertising that you could use to publicise your events?

The aim was to be as evangelistic as possible in an intimate setting without forcing the faithless to profess faith; they had to sit and listen, and that was it. In the end a large number were swaying and singing to the church youth band led worship. We asked an older member of the youth group to share some of his testimony along with the mother of a young person who had recently been completely and miraculously healed of breast cancer. A youth preacher gave a 5 minute evangelistic talk based around The Simpsons and ending with people committing their lives to Christ. By divine appointment a crew of hip hop dancers then turned up at the end to give an impromptu performance. The response was astonishing, with young people who had never applauded the gospel tentatively sticking their hands in the air, uttering Jesus as something other than a curse, and leaving perceptibly wanting more.

The future

So on the one hand we have opportunities to provide positive and proactive activities for young people through W6 and on the other we have an open channel into the church through the urban youth ministry being set up as local young people join the church and become part of building a youth congregation relevant to them and their friends. We are seeking to provide as many ways as possible for cross-over ventures between the church and the charity to make way for the gospel to be shared and heard. That's not to say that just because some young people are directionless and bored we're going to ensnare them with the gospel, it's to show, just like the Methodist church did through starting football clubs, that we care, that we're about more than pews and hymns and that we have something to offer that's holistic and enriching. Music, like football, offers one of the most attractive points of crossover, but there are many different points of contact and connection. At each stage we may need to find new ones, but for us at the moment music, both via the Vibe and the youth worship event, is proving fruitful. I know of other churches locally who are investing in football, gym classes, prophetic prayer, computer clubs and many others.

**What are the potential crossover points in your context?
How might you develop these further?**

We are an urban mission church so just providing a church babysitting service doesn't wash and it certainly doesn't work: even the youth who are forced to come by their parents resent it! It's important not to eradicate liturgy, the sacraments, service, tithing and other spiritual disciplines but in whatever we do we need to be turning theology into practicality. It means taking a Christian youth group and turning it into a mission to the local youth groups and it means wanting the unchurched youth group to become an unconventional church group. Our long road has started with music of the worship and the street variety, will continue with a fledgling youth church and alpha group, will hopefully get strengthened through prayer, unity and community and then train others in transformative prayer, worship and mission to the next generation.

Challenges and chances

All of what's been said proves how small scale the youth congregations of even large churches can be and how voluminous the problems for cross-over ministry are – and we haven't even come round the first bend of seeing urban youth ministry done effectively. We are starting a youth alpha on the back of growth this year which will provide fresh challenges but it's worth making the mistakes and experiencing the failures to learn what works and what doesn't and to keep on pressing on prayerfully. A commitment by the whole church to see youth work well established in the local area is essential, and, arguably, partnerships both secular and non are tremendously helpful, but it's still down to key leaders and a growing breed of urban youth workers, missionaries and evangelists who are there for the long term to make it happen. This is another of the reasons training young people now in urban mission is so valuable because they'll be there for the next generation.

As most people are aware, one-off events, outreaches and missions soon dry up without long term investment and relationships. One important aspect of sticking it out indefinitely is undoubtedly prayer, both for the events but also for those running the events. Belonging to a community of area and church youth workers has been really helpful for prayer, ideas, intervention and participation. And equally the searching out of God's will is crucial to making sure we're investing our time, resources and prayer into the right things. I have learnt a huge amount about looking at what the enemy's schemes are to distract us and rob our young people of their rightful access to a loving relationship with God the father. This requires us spending time with God asking him to show the hidden schemes and for us to refresh ourselves in His presence. Sometimes in the joined up thinking we forget we see the world differently, and must have courage to speak up prophetically for the young people both inside and outside of the church and take our stand against the world, the flesh and the devil.

Do you have a supportive, praying community around you? If you feel isolated where might you look to start to develop such a support network?

I believe planting a youth congregation from the inner core of the current church youth group means realigning the church's centre of gravity into the community and back to the people Jesus came to serve. A key factor is leadership and as much as we want to grow leaders from the next generation we also have to grow ourselves in faith, in confidence and in the conviction that we have a message of hope and life, and that God's kingdom will come if we humble ourselves and pray.

For further reflection ...

Lucy Hawes says that at St. Paul's Hammersmith they have a vision to see "the unchurched youth group become an unconventional church group."

If God were to move dramatically among the unchurched young people in your area and they were to create their own church what would it look like?

How would it resemble and how would it differ from the churches that currently exist?

What would a worship service look like?

CHAPTER SIX

Sharing Spiritual Gifts

Reflections on spirituality and young people at the margins

Alan Michael

There is a vast amount of material written about working or ministering with young people on the margins, about a theology or spirituality for youth work and youth workers, and about strategies for outreach work and befriending 'difficult' teens. There are also a great many resources for working with children in Church and ways of talking about God with young Christians. However, I have found a huge gap in terms of how we help our disaffected youth to explore and discover their spiritual being, and to grow in their experience of the sacred.

Is there an area of your ministry practice that seems to be untouched in the published ministry resources? Might you have something to contribute?

The group of people that I have set out to write about are vulnerable young people on the margins of British society, alienated and excluded from mainstream society and education (as well as the Church), who are involved in, or are on the verge of being, involved in criminal and anti-social behaviour. The underpinning questions I have are how do we as the Church respond to young people in this category who are desperate to be understood, accepted and taken seriously? Rather than just looking at how we might get them into Church, how can we share with them the joys of Christ so that they can experience at first-hand a relationship with Jesus in the life of the Spirit? Therefore, what I want to talk about in this chapter is my personal experience as a Franciscan Brother of being alongside young people on their journey in three different contexts: gang culture, prison ministry and school mentoring.

I have lived and ministered on three estates in different parts of Britain, all unique and yet sharing many similarities. The first of these we will focus on is an estate on Tyneside that had a very bad reputation from the day it was built to house families from the docks. There are stories still told about how the people were deloused before moving into their new homes, and so there is a stigma attached to living on the estate. The estate received a lot of bad press after the riots in 1991 and has suffered greatly from high unemployment, gangs, drugs and joy riding.

Are there stories, urban-legends or myths told about the young people of your area that affect their self-image either positively or negatively?

The Society of St Francis (SSF) moved there for a short period in 1995, living in one of the council houses. What struck me was the number of gangs of young people who wandered aimlessly around the estate in all kinds of weather and until very late at night, some being as young as 7 or 8. These were not like the tribal territorial gangs that I had come across in Glasgow but were gangs made up of extended families and friends. Our first job was befriending them, which was not difficult as they swooped on our house as soon as we arrived – who were these 'outsiders' in strange robes (habits) who set up a chapel in their house? We were bombarded with questions about faith, celibacy, sex, God, prayer, Jesus, the Church and of course sex again! There was no need to go out looking for ministry as it came to us.

Our response was to exercise a ministry of hospitality and within a week we had at least 30 youngsters a day coming to chat, play cards and drink tea. They came in varying degrees of soberness, and not only drugs, but glue-sniffing were huge problems among the younger element. However, the questions did not stop, and gradually the groups found themselves in Chapel either wanting to be prayed for or to listen to the prayers. We noticed that there was a difference between the boys and the girls. The girls wanted to sing choruses and pray out loud. The boys would not take part in this, but were more attracted to the service of Compline[1] which we sung by candlelight; the girls did not like this because they claimed it was 'spooky'. It would be easy to surmise that perhaps the boys were more embarrassed about expressing their faith (and there might have been something of that in it) but the quiet chanting and intercessions did seem to touch the lads at a very deep level, and it was they who came back night after night during our time on the estate. On occasion the Brothers would have to say Compline three times a night because of different groups wanting to join us at different times!

Do you see differences in what appeals to the different sexes? Are you able to balance your offer to give something for everyone or have you chosen a particular focus?

It would have been so easy to set up a 'class' for young people to learn about the faith, or to herd them to Church (although it would probably have had to have been in the evening – they didn't do mornings), but is this what they wanted? Would this lead them to a personal relationship with Christ? Amongst them, as with the other groups, there was a mistrust of the Church; it was seen as an institution, a place of authority, and another place that would tell them what to do and think. The Chapel on the estate belonged to the young people; the experience of Christ in that place, whatever that was, was their own experience. Yes, the Brothers were there to pray with and for them, but not to preach at them. Borgman talks in his book *Agenda for Youth Ministry* about how the Church often produces a 'flawed educational model of discipleship' where young people are disabled by being talked at. What is important to young people is identity and relationship, which is why they have such loyalty to their gangs, and therefore Borgman states in another book that "our presentation of the faith must be Christocentric rather than bibliocentric or theocentric. Adolescent Christian spirituality should be centred not on an institution but on a relationship with Jesus Christ as Saviour, Lord, and friend."[2]

We would all say that discipleship is about Christ but what does the style and method of our discipleship practice say about what we consider to most important? Are our methods sometimes better suited to producing correct knowledge, correct allegiance, correct behaviour or even correct appearance than mature relationship with Christ?

My hope is that they found this relationship with Jesus in our Chapel. Most of the youngsters were from extremely poor families, but I have never met so many youngsters that grasped so quickly what we were about and taught me about what it is to trust in Christ! The spirituality we found there was very much in the category of 'transformative' for them and for us.

The second context I have explore is through my current work in two secondary schools in Birmingham as a 'behaviour mentor' with groups of boys between the ages of 14-16 who have either low self-esteem or behavioural problems and are close to being excluded. My remit from the schools is to encourage good behaviour and participation and to challenge and change bad behaviour. I used to be told the particular reason each pupil was in the group so that I could 'do something about it', but now I prefer to start off cold, not knowing the individual reasons. This is because I soon learned that most of the youngsters were on the bottom of the pile, they felt that they were not listened to, ignored or labelled as 'trouble' and so of course they often played out that role. What I saw before me were spiritual beings that were locked in on themselves, youngsters full of life but not knowing how to express themselves fully or appropriately.

My approach was, therefore, to start from scratch, asking them what they thought: what they thought of school, adults, life; what they liked and disliked; what it was like for them growing up where they lived; and what they thought their problems were at school. This different approach helped them to open up and build up trust in the group and with myself. Each group ended up working on different projects that helped them to participate more fully in school life, from designing a school board game to meeting with the Head to talk about issues at the school. I do not believe that this was a secular role, but in the 'formative' category was very spiritual as well, and liberating in terms of empowering the young people. The youngsters were sharing their thoughts and feelings at a very deep level. As a result of one of these groups opening up about their fears and anxieties, there came the use of relaxation exercises and guided meditations, which I have used with each group since. However, it is not something that can be imposed on the group, but has to almost come from them; when and if they come to the point where they open up and share their vulnerabilities it can be offered to them as a tool. Once in my enthusiasm I tried to introduce it too quickly and it was a complete disaster! I know that some of the staff that pass by the room I use are amazed at the stillness that is evident from groups that are at other times often loud and boisterous. It is not surprising to me though that, once taught how to be still and silent, young people will grasp and cherish this reality; they live very busy lives, more and more pressure seems to be put on pupils today, they receive information from all directions and so to be able to be still and quiet is a breath of fresh air to them.

One example of a meditation exercise that I use is getting them to picture themselves on holiday on a beach, including who they would take with them, etc. Then they have to think about the people they have left behind and to think about the good qualities of those people. This simple meditation had a huge and significant effect on one youngster – he lived alone with his mum and had in the meditation left her behind. He later talked about how he began to see that he took her for granted and since then he has continued to help her with some of the housework each week! Often youngsters can fail to see the bigger picture and feel that life revolves round them. Being in touch spiritually helps them see the needs of others and to find their place in the world. Borgman argues that those ministering to youth need to understand the post-modern world: He writes: "Theology arising from contact with young people looks at life from within a youth culture shaped by contemporary thought and mass media. In this post-Christian and post-modern era many have rejected Christian values; for them moral authorities have lost their appeal, reason and science their credibility. Logical systems, theological proofs, and legitimate authority no longer count…A pluralistic and secular society is either too busy or disinclined to ask: What is the meaning of life? What is truth? What determines right and wrong? Why are we doing what we are doing? Where are we headed? We must find ways to make these questions once again relevant and basic to young people."[3] I believe that meditation can be one way to pose those questions.

Have you found helpful ways of giving young people space and encouragement to ask the 'big questions'?

The final area I want to outline is the work I undertook as a chaplain for a couple of years at a YOI (Young Offender Institution). During that time I was asked to lead weekends at other YOIs for inmates who were either recent converts or were looking at the Christian faith. I was under no illusion that sometimes to become a Christian in prison can be to play the system, it looks good at a parole board hearing! However, this is not to deny that many do make a lasting commitment and, after all, if someone is there for the wrong reason they still may find something in the Chaplaincy that they hadn't expected!

The inmates were the same type of youngsters that I had encountered on the estates but a bit further down the line in terms of the criminal system. Prison already gives youngsters plenty of opportunities to think because of the amount of time that they are locked away on their own in their cells, so often they will have begun to ponder questions, such as those Borgman lists above, that would not naturally occur to them in other settings, and so those who took part in the spirituality weekends brought a lot with them in terms of seeking after truth and asking about faith.

St. Augustine prayed "My heart is restless, until it finds its rest in you O Lord". How true this is for all of us, and it is a prayer that many young people on the weekends could identify with. What they yearned for was to be accepted, to be wanted, to be loved, to be fulfilled. Many acknowledged that they had looked in the wrong places for this – to drugs, alcohol, gangs, stealing or sex (which was where Augustine had himself turned) – but none of these things had brought peace or happiness.

If we begin by telling young people that what they are doing is wrong they will instantly switch off. On the other hand if we begin by offering them something greater than what they already have or know about then perhaps they will at least look into it themselves. Therefore, weekends were designed to be both 'formative and transformative'. We began where they were at, asking them to tell their stories, which were often both tragic and humbling at the same time. Alongside their stories we would look at stories from the Bible, stories of love, of courage, of liberation. From both sets of stories and through the telling of them came penitence and healing.

Often young people who live chaotic and dysfunctional lives carry around with them a lot of baggage, hurts and guilt from the past which they do not know how to deal with appropriately. This is where the Church can offer help, acceptance of responsibilities, forgiveness and healing. This should lead us into not just talking about God but into experiencing God's presence through meditation. In the introduction to *Tune In, Chill Out*, Jenny Baker claims that "young people, like all of us, need time and space to be with God. They are searching for encounters with God that have depth and meaning. They don't want to be entertained or patronised. They want the real thing, and in contemplative prayer, that is what they get."[4] It was incredibly moving to watch people changing over so short a period of time as they began or deepened their relationship with God.

Would you have enough confidence in this style of ministry to use these contemplative methods with a normally boisterous group of young people? Why or why not?

These three cases are perhaps unique to my ministry and calling...but the need to engage young people in similar situations is not unique to me or to any context. So what can exploring Christian spirituality in general offer to young people living on the margins who are searching for meaning in their lives?

- We need to be able to offer a listening ear. We need to help them to grow in maturity by listening to themselves, to others and to God.
- We must accompany them in humility, willing to go to where they are and be willing to learn about God from them.
- We can offer them relationship with Jesus, a relationship that offers healing, forgiveness, acceptance, empowerment and fulfilment.
- They can discover purpose in life as well as self-discipline and responsibility.

This last point is highlighted by the recent report "Spiritual Health and Well Being of Urban Young People", which has very strong evidence pointing to the fact that young people who pray and are in touch with their spirituality are much more focussed in life and "are much more likely to find life worth living."[5]

All of this is well summed up in the book *Accompanying* in which the authors describe how the spiritual life is like a gift in a wrapped box: "It is within us, but we do need to bring it out of its box and assemble it so that we can use it, experience and enjoy it. When we are young and inexperienced, it is not always easy to open our gifts or to assemble them ourselves and we need a helping hand from someone who, though recognising that it is our gift, helps us to unpack and assemble it and then leaves us alone to enjoy it. That is how God acts in the story of creation after he gives us his spirit. He puts us in charge (Genesis 1:28)."[6]

Notes

1 Compline is a form of evening prayer
2 Borgman: 1997 pg xiv
3 Borgman:1997 pg 25
4 Baker & Ratnayake: 2004 pg 7
5 Rees, Francis & Robbins: 2005 pg 16
6 Green & Christian: 1998 pg 8

For further reflection ...

At the beginning of his account Fr Alan Michael speaks of a "huge gap" in the published resources when it comes to helping "disaffected youth to explore and discover their spiritual being, and to grow in their experience of the sacred". This chapter is a step towards plugging that gap.

Is there an area of your work and practice that seems untouched by published youth work or youth ministry resources?

Might you have something to contribute to fill this gap? If so, contact us at Youthwork the Partnership with your thoughts and ideas.

CHAPTER SEVEN

Tough Estate, Superkids

Holy Spirit Church and Ferrier Focus

Mick Russell, Helen Russell and Daphne Clifton

The Ferrier Estate is a deprived, concrete-built district of 1960s homes built in squares and tower blocks in South Greenwich, London. It has got worse recently owing to a bogus regeneration scheme, leaving it pock-marked with empty properties, most of them with windows removed and replaced with a nylon mesh that allows cold and damp to affect neighbouring homes. The estate is characterised by high unemployment and struggling lone parents. Typical of the area is the young, lone mother under huge pressures, usually unaided by a partner or instead hindered by his psychological baggage, and often later abandoned. Drugs or alcohol are often a means of emotional escape.

The ethnic mix is 50-60% BME (Black and Minority Ethnic). In addition to the other problems experienced in the community,[1] refugee families are affected by the enormous traumas of losing loved ones – in the case of Somalis, often it is the father, the authority figure in the family, who has been killed by warring militias – and being uprooted and transplanted into a totally different culture. The results are psychological damage and profound pain.

Lawrence Singlehurst described mission as being in three phases- 'Sowing, Reaping and Keeping'. However, where experience of life is so negative, it is necessary to add a prior, fourth phase – "preparing the ground" for the seed. The whole mission on the Ferrier Estate has adopted the 'Belonging, Believing, Behaving' model, with the addition of 'Blessing' – preparing the ground, as it were – with most activities focused on Blessing. The ground has been hardened historically by generations of exploitation, deprivation and social exclusion, which led to community and family disintegration and (arguably) has initiated a cycle of emotional damage passed from one generation to another; I believe the roots of anti-social activity lie here.[2]

Which stage – preparing the ground; sowing; reaping; keeping – do you spend most of your time on?

The work we undertake on the Ferrier estate, organised around the Holy Spirit Church, is wide and varied, touching both young and old. However, in this piece we want to focus on two aspects of our work which aim to break the cycles of damage I have mentioned above – Superkidz and Gang Time.

The Superkidz Project has its origins in a club called 'Coconut Club', a primary school outreach which was run by Eltham Green Christian Centre. In 1998 they decided to move this club to the Ferrier Estate, which they had become passionate about serving after years of prayer for the area. Supported by the local Anglican Vicar, the club's leader Helen Lodge and another mission leader, Debbie Charles, moved into the church flat on the estate, which had been left in a sordid state by squatters.[3] To tackle the particular needs of the estate, Helen implemented a model pioneered by Kidz Klub with fast-moving, messy games, funky worship songs and culturally relevant Gospel talks, supported by the crucial weekly home visits to every child on the register in order to develop relationships with them and their families. My wife Helen Russell, who took the leadership of Superkidz over, in 2001, picks up the story later. However, before coming to that I want to introduce our work with gangs.

When, as a Church Army officer, I first came to live and work here in 1999, my future wife Helen and I did a door-to-door survey which revealed that most people feared the youth gangs who had nothing to do but engage in car-crime, robbery and drug-dealing. In the mission team we therefore consciously focused on youth and children's work. Initially we suffered from some threats, vandalism and thefts, with lighted newspaper coming through our letter box and setting off the smoke alarms, and sometimes urine, along with graffiti on the door itself (sometimes graphically insulting to Helen). Over the years my wife and I got to know the more difficult young people, and our home on the estate was a place they came for meals, for Christian seeker courses, and in one case, accommodation when his mother (an addict) was evicted. He had become a Christian through one of our clubs but lapsed into drug using and dealing. He is now in prison serving a sentence for armed robbery, witnessing to others, in spite of some spiritual ups and downs.

Broadly, there are black gangs and a white gang, though all would see themselves as "Ferrier", particularly in the face of aggression by gangs from other areas in the borough. Drug dealing is a major feature of the lives of the young men who attend our activities and the beatings and (mainly) superficial stabbings go with failure to pay drug debts. From time to time the violence gets out of hand and in June 2007 there was a near fatal stabbing, resulting in four boys now facing a charge of attempted murder, because one of their number has deep psychological problems and went mad during a fight to defend a younger friend. There are many tragic stories associated with this kind of work, and some encouraging ones, one of which is included as a conclusion to this chapter.

Superkidz

Helen Russell

In the summer of 2001, I was attending a mission committee meeting when it was announced that the club for primary-aged young people we had been developing on the Ferrier Estate would be closing due to the departure of the most recent voluntary leader. Much to my horror, the next agenda item was immediately announced. I interrupted, exclaiming that the demise of the club would be a tragedy, and it is at that moment I believe God called me to lead Superkidz. My outburst ultimately resulted in my transformation into a fully-blown children's and youth worker!

I took over leadership almost immediately, setting aside about two days a week from my full-time voluntary mission work here. Although I had already been part of the Superkidz team for a year, I was instantly overwhelmed by the amount of detailed preparation that went into each Saturday's extravaganza, from finding wacky props and organising the weekly visits to 160 children, to fronting the frenzy of fun! Overnight, I went from being a shy background team member to discovering the wilder side of my personality which was rapidly emerging! This new found freedom and God-given equipping was exhilarating and prompted some creative initiatives. I hosted the first of many Superkidz family parties in December 2001, during which kids played messy games alongside their carers, watched a Gospel magic show courtesy of Nick, my multi-talented husband, and much to their delight each received a Christmas present donated by partner churches.

The end-of-term parties quickly contributed to the growing number of families we visited and at our peak we were visiting 340 children weekly. Another volunteer, Helen Peevor, joined me and we each spent four hours a week visiting children and their families and developing friendships with them. Gradually we were invited in for a cup of tea, sometimes in deeply impoverished conditions. Abuse, domestic violence, relationship breakdowns and 'drugs beatings' soon became familiar subjects and our eyes were opened to the suffering that went on behind closed doors. We were amazed at the resilience of many young people who had been through traumas of parental loss due to untimely death or imprisonment and endured streams of interchangeable step-fathers or ordeals with substance-addicted family members. We began to meet needs as they arose: distributing food, accessing grants and advocating on behalf of their families, supporting mums in crisis and offering Bible studies to those expressing an interest in faith. This non-authoritarian model of friendship-based family support has given us opportunities to work with countless families that were intimidated by statutory services.

The time and energy devoted to the visits in this model is remarkable; how might such a commitment impact your work?

In the summer of 2002, I identified a need for a youth club for Superkidz 'graduates' and 'Chill Out Zone' began in our home. The twelve or so young people enjoyed the homely atmosphere which characterised the club. Indeed, one girl who lived with her mentally ill mother likened the club to a family. We would celebrate each young person's birthday with a themed party of their choice and, surprisingly, many traditional childhood games like musical statues were enjoyed by the teenagers! However, some members teetered on the edge of social exclusion, playing truant and engaging in small-time crime. The club's comparatively low-key activities of cooking, crafts and issues-based work appeared to provide a welcome break from the isolation of wandering the streets or enduring family unrest at home and at the end individuals would sometimes hide in cupboards or under beds, saying they wished they lived here with us. Two years on, the weekly thefts of shoes and generous smatterings of pizza daubed upon our walls became too much to bear and we moved to the church, evolving into a Rock Solid club (a Youth for Christ model) on the way. We extended day trips to residential weekends when we developed links with an adventure centre, whose staff, although more used to middle class youth groups, graciously accommodated our motley crew! Since then we have opened GirlZone, which builds on this youth work, reaching out to girls at risk of participation in underage and coercive sex with multiple partners, drug dealing and violence, all of which are so prevalent in the gang scene here.

In the first year of assuming leadership of Superkidz, I had undertaken the tiresome yet essential tasks of writing policies, budgets and a constitution and forming a management committee. The work had now become a full-time role and I found myself running a fledgling project with accountability to St. James PCC. This, in combination with an unpredictable home ministry to people in crisis and a steady stream of young visitors, was draining. I felt duty-bound to ensure that the project would not perish through lack of leadership in the future, believing that paid staff would add greater security in the long-term. Reluctantly I acknowledged that if the project was to be sustainable, I should enter the fearsome world of fundraising!

Over the next eighteen months we secured only a few thousand pounds towards a youth worker's salary, as most funders politely declined. However, in early 2004, I read from Isaiah 30 v 23, "He will send rain for the seed you sow in the ground." I had a strong sense that the rain represented funding for the seeds of truth we were sowing through the project. Hesitantly, I pinned this verse on my office wall, barely sure whether I could believe it. Within days the full £5,000 deficit required to fund a part-time youth worker was donated anonymously! Since then the money has not stopped flowing and my wavering faith has been strengthened as I have repeatedly seen Him fulfil His promises. The upshot is that Anthony Powell has been our full-time youth worker since November 2005.

God has also proved faithful in His provision of voluntary staff who have sacrificed Saturday lie-ins to pitch up to Superkidz, visit the kids whatever the weather and work at our other clubs. Indeed, without them the project would be unable to function. In the summer of 2002, as the first batch of my inherited team embarked on gap years, got married or simply needed a break, I began to lose faith in God's ability to keep the project afloat, until I had a revelation! I read an exhortation to thank Him in advance and, more importantly, in faith for the team He was going to send.

Chastened, I began this in earnest and since then we have been sent an abundance of new people at timely intervals; professionals, young people and local parents.

Inspired by a talk given by Ann Morisey on Catalyst Trust's 'Urban Mission Toolkit' course in 2003, I eagerly invited our first local non-Christian mum to join the team. Although it seemed risky, it was a pivotal decision. I could see the lady was open to the Gospel, having initially been drawn by the love the team had shown her children during the visits to her home. As her diary filled up with various Project commitments, including attending our Management Committee meetings and Superkidz, she became a key link with her neighbours, recruiting and accompanying several kids each week to our different clubs. It was a joy a short time later to hear her explain to one of our funders that the project had given her life a purpose and that she had now come to faith! Over the years several mums, including a Muslim, have joined the team; sharing in team life and moving closer to God. On one occasion, two mums who were deeply moved during a 'listening prayer' team training session, described in non-church language how Jesus had spoken to them. Such opportunities would have been totally missed if we had adhered to a strict "Christian-only" team policy.

Might there be opportunities in your context to draw people into close contact with a Christian community through utilising the time and gifts they have to offer?

Similarly, our junior team, formed in 2002, is constituted mainly of Superkidz graduates, many of whom are grappling with faith issues. Although the wild behaviour of thefts, roof-jumping and on-stage fighting has often exasperated us, it has been rewarding to see progress in individuals. They have learned technical, presentation, drama and co-operation skills, whilst being exposed to Gospel truths at Superkidz. We build upon this by undertaking one-to-one work with particularly troubled young people manifesting challenging behaviour. For example, over five years of much mentoring and discipline, a once aggressive and fearful girl has experienced unconditional love and heard God's whispers. This lovely young woman is now an adult team member and has been welcomed into a local church! Our recent partnership with Catalyst Trust has enabled us to formalise such work through its COACH mentoring scheme, in which young people and families are partnered with a coach to empower them to take steps to pursue their aspirations. She is now matched with a coach to walk alongside her as she embarks upon her childcare training.

In 2003 I developed friendships with some young people from St. James' Church and invited them to visit the Ferrier Estate. Although just half a mile away from the relative suburbia of the Blackheath borders where they lived, the estate had always been a "no-go" zone, but they rose to the challenge! Unfortunately, as I showed them round the estate, an unidentified object was hurled out of the upstairs window of an apparently derelict house, shattering glass about us! (Not that this compared to a previous team walkabout, when Nick and I were shown a machete by the terrified mother of a gang member we were working with, who had threatened her with decapitation!) However, despite the immense cultural differences, the St. James' youth immersed themselves in Superkidz with great gusto, revelling in the opportunity to lead from the front and stamp their mark upon the events. The combination of the enormous amount of fun we have each Saturday and the personal and spiritual nurturing we provide has been an attractive marketing feature which has been naturally employed in recruiting from other church youth groups. This has resulted in friendships and (inevitably) romance across the borough! For many, the flame of passion for the poor that was first lit when they began working here as teenagers still burns brightly. Two former volunteers have gone on to write dissertations about the impact of regeneration upon the community and Alana Daly, a member of St. James, is a wonderful asset as a full-time project worker.

My personal vision statement, which hangs on my office wall is "to spend my life loving, valuing and empowering broken people whom the world has forgotten". At times, I have wept as God has revealed the depths of brokenness that some people here experience and this has strengthened my determination to walk alongside them and to see young people and their families flourish despite the problems, both within their homes and externally, on the estate. (This has not been painless – encouragement and prayer through urban mission networks has been crucial to persevere in the isolation and often relentless demands that living and serving on an estate entail.) Whilst the definitive fulfilment of my vision is for people to know Jesus as Saviour through our Gospel-based work, I believe that those who partake of the kingdom of God through new opportunities, and the resulting released potential, experience something of eternal significance that cannot ultimately leave them untouched.

In practice, therefore, I have extended the work beyond Christian and moral programmes, teaching about the dangers of things such as drugs, crime and joy-riding. For example, the netball club has propelled young people into competitive sport and our residential trips offer new opportunities away from the estate's confines, while family parties and "Supermumz Nites" have demonstrated God's desire for fullness of life. Moreover, central to the success of the project is the development of healthy relationships with the young people in which they feel valued, which does not fit neatly into grant feedback forms. We demonstrate this by spending time listening to them at the bus stop, in the chip shop or on the way to school. It can easily take me an hour simply to pop downstairs to the shops! One of the key things I highlight to the team is speaking truth into the young people at every available opportunity, not only to build up self-esteem but also to counteract the lies spoken over some of them; that they are worthless and have no future. (Once, as I cooed over her newborn baby, a mother of four declared, "Babies are OK for the first year but then I get sick of the sight of them".) Instead we tell them how wonderful they are, notice their new shoes and encourage them to follow their dreams.

It is a sad fact that in order to see young people flourish, I inevitably get involved in child protection cases. Aside from the emotional impact, this comes with a more worrying cost. I have lost friendships and been threatened as a result of referrals I have made to Social Services when children have been in danger. Although God has turned critical situations around miraculously, the fear of intimidation has become harder to bear since the birth of our daughter. As part of the community here, we cannot retreat to a home safely away from potential threats – many people are able to point others in the direction of our flat! One girl threatened to put lit newspaper through our letterbox and set light to my hair, and shortly afterwards "Helen is a bitch" was scrawled in permanent marker on our car. (We cannot afford to dismiss threats of arson as we have been targeted before.) In this instance, when the social worker visited me, she was amazed to hear positive things about the girl and her siblings and asked me to document them for a multi-disciplinary meeting. Remarkably, within a week our relationship with the family was restored and we continue to offer support. Not all relationships are restored, however.

What resources can you draw upon and what support networks can you turn to when things are hard? If you've nowhere to turn, how might you develop this kind of relationship?

Having lived and walked alongside so many young people over the past eight years, it is heart-breaking to see some of them make destructive life choices despite the truth they have heard and seen in action. Girls have become pregnant in their teens and several lads whom Superkidz visited for years and who were once club members, are now immersed in the world of crime and gang culture. In 2005 I was called as a court witness after one of several interventions in muggings and attacks. The violent assault was perpetrated by lads that we have taken on trips and entertained in our home. (Relationships were amazingly restored with both young men despite my "betrayal" and one of them refers to us as his family!) However, for many years I have hung on to the thought that prison will offer hope to some of these lads when the inevitable happens. Indeed, prison has enabled some young men to find God, partly through a combination of the chaplains' and our mission team's follow-up support. Two lads in whom Nick and I have heavily invested are now seeing their childhood faith rekindled in prison, and seeds sown many years ago are beginning to bear fruit. It is a wonderfully humbling moment when roles are reversed and you are the recipient of a Bible study from a lad behind bars!

We cannot claim to have seen a major revival within the community here. Only a handful of young people are now engaged in local churches where they are being nurtured. Yet I have seen prayers answered, children worshipping God and lives committed to Him. We have lost over a hundred children since the regeneration's de-cant process began, but are undertaking follow up work with some families who have moved off the estate. We have been able to introduce some mothers and their children to Ferrier Friendship Tea, Holy Spirit Church's informal Fresh Expressions service and Coffee Stop, its adult weekday drop-in. For most, perhaps the transition to a church setting is a step too far. The development of our Mums' café at Superkidz, however, seems to be less threatening and it is wonderful to see mums dancing with the children in the worship time. Indeed I regard Superkidz as an expression of church, planted right in the heart of the community. Seeds of truth have undoubtedly been sown in the lives of the few hundred who have attended our clubs over the past 9 years. I am therefore content that whether or not I see fruit this side of heaven, "He who has begun a good work in them is faithful to complete it..."

The "Gang Time" Drop-in

We started a drop-in specifically for gang members because they became too violent and difficult to fit into 'normal' youth activities. There are reasons for this, which psychologists such as Bowlby discuss[4]. In a nut shell though, it means that the word "love" can literally have little meaning for our gang members. This problem is met in an extraordinarily focused way by Christian youth work: God's persevering love channelled through His people in practical action and relationships. In these practical ways socially excluded young people learn about that love and experience it. It is an expression of the infinite value God places on each individual: a powerful antidote to deep feelings of worthlessness, reinforced by inability to concentrate and by failure at school, by negative role models and the dominating culture of the lawless gang (often described by the young people as a surrogate family). It is also a liberating force for the young people who feel anxious and constrained to put on a hard front, to conceal their real personalities, to conform to negative group norms, and to spend ill-gotten money on designer clothes as a means to identity.

It is not easy to find people who are able to live with the volatile behaviour, bad language and theft and vandalism that goes with youth work of this sort. Daphne Clifton was a "natural", instantly relating to the young people as she took her turn as 'bouncer' in the team on the church door. She quickly began to be heavily involved, and to make an enormously valuable contribution, along with our other team members, who included our Baptist Minister, Charlie Ingram, stepping in for a considerable time until the team grew sufficiently.

Daphne, Helen and I persevere in visiting and writing to our members when they are in prison, and this is often a time when they reflect on where they are, and come into contact with the excellent work done by prison chaplains.

In 2004, Sarah Ingram, who had done excellent work with gang members in 2000 with Greenwich Youth for Christ, returned with our Baptist Minister Charlie and began the predecessor to the Skills Club, which was based on the 'Life Worth Living' course, and later set up the Violence Intervention Project to tackle the root causes of youth violence and crime at an early developmental stage, also under GYFC (now headed by Hugh Ridsdill-Smith, who succeeded Nick Shepherd, the editor of this book). To ensure best practice I decided also to do gang work under GYFC.

With Daphne, I started the second phase of the Skills Club for gang members, based on the theme of motorcycle mechanics to try and encourage an interest in literacy and numeracy, and also on car washing to earn legitimate money. The third version of the Skills Club is more geared towards employment, and Daphne leads it with her enormously valuable business gifts and experience and her knowledge of local commerce.

This work has clearly developed through a number of phases. Has your work also developed or is it static? If it is static, is this because it is effective, or should you be looking for the next step?

After four years, the church is no longer a target of vandalism and theft, and we can trust the young people we know. We hear about violence meted out to members of other gangs, and robberies continue to be a problem, though I believe less so as a result of a decreased feeling of alienation from the rest of society, and the beginnings of a new willingness to be real and vulnerable, and to be more humane to outsiders.

Daphne describes her striking work with one particular young person below. I am convinced that Daphne's work with this young man has actually saved other people from serious injury or even death, as well as releasing him to be the person he was created truly to be.

Steve's story

Daphne Clifton

Standing outside a shop front Church in all weathers isn't most people's idea of fun youth work and my early involvement of making sandwiches for tea moved to engagement with the lads. 'Engage' probably isn't the term most people would choose for this type of detached youth work – managing a siege is probably a better description. In my naivety, and with only my youth work experience having been in traditional, clean C of E Sunday Schools, I used my usual style of "sit down, be quiet, have a drink and eat some food." I think they were shocked at being spoken to normally (in my posh, white, middle class accent) and some of the lads did as I asked. But not for long! Their methods of terrorising soon took over and their almost feral behaviour got the better of them. If something moved, it was fair game for either throwing or stealing it and if it didn't move, brute force would soon change that. The times that they were quiet and obedient were fun for me; listening to their chatter and trying to engage with them.

I loved those boys and the fraught times we spent together on a Sunday afternoon. We couldn't allow the lads to take over the Church but neither did we want to exclude them from Church and God's love, so it was agreed that two of us would remain outside the Church with the door locked each week. That way, those inside would be free to enjoy their tea and we could engage with the lads. How the lads loved the challenge of trying to get past us and in to the Church! More than once the adults inside had to leave via the back door, which then gave the lads a second point of entry to enjoy.

When Nick told me I had a 'real gift' with the lads, I was surprised, as I thought everyone loved badly behaved teenage boys. I'm so thankful to him for having the wisdom to point that out to me; it was a real turning point for me and following that, one lad in particular.

One sunny Sunday afternoon, the usual banter was going on outside the Church with the lads and I was standing with my back to the door. There's a letter box in the glass door just below waist height and I could see a fountain of 'water' flowing in on to the mat the other side. Steve was facing and pressed up against the letter box. It was pretty obvious what he was trying to make me think he was doing and I noted it verbally, giggled and let the behaviour pass. As Steve came away from the door he held a Kiaora carton in his hand; now empty. What a laugh!

I'm told I was the first adult able to engage with Steve, an extremely violent lad who had beaten up more than one youth worker in the past and was under arrest for some misdemeanour or other most weeks. One week Steve was bemoaning the fact that his knuckle-duster-like gold ring was broken and I offered to have it fixed as I was due to go to the jeweller for a new watch battery. "Would you? I ain't got no money" was his response. "Take it as an early birthday present" was all he needed to agree to hand the ring over. A couple of weeks later I returned the ring in all its glory, with a note requesting him not to use it as a knuckle duster in future. He was pleased.

These casual Sunday interactions moved to the Thursday Skills club. Steve joined in the car cleaning and cooking with enthusiasm and a fair amount of choice language. Trust was building, which eventually led to me supporting him on trips to Court. That's another whole story – suffice to say that the lads viewed this as a great day out together, with a trip on the train, some new shops to raid and a trip to the Golden Arches for lunch! I used to pay for what I knew about and apologise to shop keepers for what I missed. "Hey Daf!" they'd shout, "we like shopping with you; can we go Up West?" The grace of God abounded. And we didn't go Up West.

Work with marginalised young people inevitably brings you into contact with anti-social and criminal behaviour. Do you think Daphne and the others writing this article have found the right balance between responsibility to the young people they work with and to the law and society at large? Would you do anything differently?

Gradually I started to speak for Steve in Court and was able, honestly, to report my experience of him as a relatively hard-working, bright lad who respected and engaged positively with me if not the rest of society. As Christian youth workers, one of our main goals is to get the lads to see and own up to the truth of their actions. I believe this is the first step they must take as they learn the meaning and application of the word 'responsibility.'

As part of introducing Steve to the world of work I took him to a meeting with my publisher as my first book was being discussed. We prepared with a 'how to prepare for meetings' session, which covered attitude, dress code and meeting etiquette. We had a fun morning out in the West End, including the meeting and a Golden Arches lunch. With no prejudice against Steve, my publisher noted how well he did in his first meeting and what a nice young lad he was. That was such an important thing for him to hear.

A couple of years after first meeting Steve, the dreaded day came. I witnessed him beat up a young lad who was a youth worker at the Thursday Drop-In Centre. What made it worse was that the lad was living with my family at the time. I had to take him to Casualty and make a witness statement. By this time I had met Steve's mother and been able to show my support for the family while she spent a few months at Her Majesty's pleasure. How on earth would I be able to face her now that I was a witness against Steve? I feared her response marginally less than that of Steve's. A week or so later, I was driving Steve home in the car and told him I'd had to be a witness but that I would still support him. "It's OK. I know you Christians have to tell the truth." What a break through as well as a relief. The case didn't come to Court for nearly a year and I went to several others with Steve in the mean time.

The inevitable happened and Steve was sent to a Young Offenders Institute with two other lads as a result of an aggravated burglary. Monthly visits ensued, with Steve proving to be a lively correspondent; his mood and thoughts both being articulated in his own, humorous style. My visits included two other lads and we all met together in the Chapel for an hour or so. I introduced prayer to our meetings and had some amazing times with God. Prison Chaplains do an amazing job!

Steve was released from a Young Offenders Institute with an ISSP (Intensive Supervision and Surveillance Programme) involving a tag and programme of attending Young Offenders Team (YOT) and the Pupil Referral Unit (PRU). Whilst on tag, attendance was fine but sadly once the tag was off he went backwards in his attendance, which resulted in a breach of his ISSP and another court appearance.

A few months before the Court appearance was due, Steve's father and his father's girlfriend came to a sticky and untimely end to their lives. It was an horrific incident and although Steve was fairly estranged from his father, blood is blood. The family were open to me attending the funeral and were happy for me to support them in any small way that I could.

The breach of ISSP is a serious offence, and prison or a heavy fine was the expected outcome. That court appearance was a tough one, with an excellent Judge who was livid with Steve for "sticking two fingers up to him and society." The Judge swung round to ask me why he shouldn't send Steve back to prison. I repeated my experiences of him being a bright young lad, who, when supervised and stretched, responds well. Steve was given a reprieve and told he had 8 weeks to mend his ways or go back to prison. The Judge was extremely cross with Steve and made it clear he was in no mood to be taken for the proverbial ride. We knew he was serious and I agreed to work closer with Steve, which involved a few public speaking lessons so that he could at least represent himself clearly in Court. The lessons were fun and involved role play – initiated by Steve. We discussed what he would say, the things he'd achieved and what he'd learned over the 8 weeks. One of the other things I did was to take Steve and his mum to visit a nun friend of mine in an Abbey. She had been praying for him for years and he'd asked to meet her. We had a lovely afternoon out in the country away from the chaos of life.

Eight weeks later, despite early hic-coughs, Steve and his mother arrived at the court. It was a long day, waiting for our slot and thankfully no-one's patience ran out. Eventually the list caller asked us to go into the Court without a solicitor, as the Judge had said Steve's was a good report and he could manage on his own, if he was in agreement.

Steve confidently agreed to appear on his own with his Mum and me. We sat before the Judge and when Steve was spoken to he rose to his feet. The Judge asked him to relax and sit down. The Judge then proceeded to be effusive in his praise for Steve following an excellent progress report from the YOT. The Judge was only too happy to hear what Steve had to say and again invited him to sit down when he rose to address the Judge.

As Steve spoke, the Judge listened intently, smiled at his achievements in practising for his driving theory test, and his comments about the estate he no longer visits and that, given his experience, the Judge had thought it a good place to stay away from. The solicitor arrived half way through Steve's talk and the Judge said, "It's OK, we don't need you, Steve's managing perfectly well on his own." The solicitor was not required to say a word for the rest of the appearance. Having listened to Steve, the Judge repeated his congratulations for the effort and results Steve had put in to the past 8 weeks. He reminded Steve that he was a man of his word and had been delighted with the reported change in him. Although giving a word of caution that Steve is very much at the beginning of a journey, the Judge wished him every success in the future. He also said, "This is the best case I've had all day." The smile on the Judge's face said it all. Steve replied clearly, "Thank you, Sir."

Steve's mum was given the opportunity of saying how she had noticed the change in him and how much that had pleased her. It all felt a bit like 'the mutual adoration society' and I was almost in tears with pride and joy throughout!

As we left the Court, the Judge called Steve back on a technical point. The Clerk of the Court had reminded him that as a result of breaching his ISSP, Steve must be given a prison sentence or fine. The Judge smiled and said, "Well, I'm not going to send you back to prison. I'll fine you £5 and remit it." (This meant Steve didn't have to pay.)

The story continues as the ISSP now comes to an end and Steve, at 16 years old, is effectively left to his own devices to find a job and make his life work. To get him this far has taken an inordinate amount of time, energy and prayer. All the young lads in a similar situation are surrounded by people telling them they are useless, when what they really need is the opposite. Blessing, Belonging, Believing and Behaving, with most activities focused on Blessing.

Notes

1 Unemployment about 28%, young lone parents with pre-schoolers comprise 25% of the families. In the 1990's the estate was 11th in the DETR deprivation rankings.

2 Many would say that the anger and violence of young people results from a destruction of family and community life and values through a number of long-term socio-economic factors: (historically) exploitative industrialisation and the splintering of families and communities; urban poverty, with a resultant minority culture of criminality.

3 We "stand on the shoulders of giants": there have been others who have done great youth work on the estate, notably two young ladies, Debbie Charles and Helen Lodge, from a local free church, Eltham Green Church. They lived in our vicarage flat on the estate and worked from there for six months before I arrived, and continued to pour in huge efforts for some time afterwards. Eltham Green Church remain major mission partners.

4 The psychologist John Bowlby researched juvenile delinquency and found that there was a correlation between problematic child-parent bonds (attachments) and criminality, and that infants form an "Internal Working Model", a kind of lens through which all other relationships are viewed in later life. This "lens" becomes very distorted by harsh experiences in infancy and childhood. In effect the child adapts beliefs and behaviour to what he or she perceives human relationships and other people to be like.

For further reflection ...

There is a large team of full-time and volunteer mission partners carrying on the work we have read about in this chapter. Sometimes the people we read about seemed 'gifted' from the start, others were equipped at they went along: "I went from being a shy background team member to discovering the wilder side of my personality."

Do you feel naturally equipped for the work you are doing with young people or do you struggle with feelings of inadequacy?

Do you believe that God can use your natural (but God-given!) gifts at the same time as he can equip you with new gifts to do all that he has called you to do?

Do you believe that God will provide the team needed to carry out his plans and purposes in your situation?

Why not make a priority of praying for God's equipping gifts for you and your team and also explore practical ways (training courses, seminars, conferences, mentoring) of developing your and your team's abilities.

CHAPTER EIGHT

Skating to the Kingdom

Making a missional impact in a youth sub-culture

Jo Dolby

Skate Outeach Manager, Bath Youth for Christ (www.one-eighty.org.uk)

Case Study – One Eighty

I was fourteen years old, skateboarding on Nottingham's Market Square with my friends as normal. Two policemen approached our group and informed us that we were not allowed to skateboard there, and, if we continued, our boards would be confiscated. I told the policeman I would stop skateboarding if he told the mountain bikers across the other side of the square to stop cycling. He told me it 'wasn't the same' and refused to continue the conversation.

A recent advertising campaign by Nike SB asked the question, "What if we treated all athletes the way we treat skateboarders?" The adverts showed runners being cursed at in the street and told to grow up, tennis players arrested for playing tennis on a tennis court and golfers having their clubs confiscated. The adverts are humorous, but their point is exceptionally powerful. Can you imagine that happening in real life? It wouldn't happen, because tennis, golf and running are socially acceptable sports. Skateboarding and skateboarders are not socially acceptable or at least are less socially acceptable than the aforementioned sports.

What is it about skateboarding that seems to annoy people so much? Why do people seem to misunderstand and reject it?

Since its beginning, skateboarding has developed from an unknown hobby created and practised by a few surfers to an internationally recognised sport and one of the largest youth sub-cultural groups in the world. The July 30th 2002 edition of 'USA Today' stated that there are approximately 12 – 18 million skateboarders in the U.S.A. alone, which is 5% of the entire population. Despite the mainstream, skateboarding has retained its 'sub culture' label. I don't want to tell you what this 'sub-culture' is like, because I will get it wrong. My experience of skate culture will be different to someone else's experience, because skate culture is made up of individuals, who can all be very different to each other.

However, it is safe to say that skate culture could be defined as young people who skate or who are linked to skaters. It is made up of mostly young people aged 11–18, it is very male dominated and can consist of people who 'don't fit' into mainstream youth culture. If you skate, you are accepted; your clothes, interests, family are irrelevant. As long as you skate, you're in.

As I grew up as both a Christian and a skateboarder, I began to get increasingly irritated about the way skateboarders were treated. What I believed about God made me sure he didn't like the way skateboarders were treated either. The bible seemed to be full of stories of God mightily using what the world saw as stupid, loving the people no one else loved, sticking up for the oppressed and marginalised. I knew I had to do something.

The idea for One Eighty came out of a need to show skateboarders that they are loved, accepted and honoured for what they do and who they are, both by people and by God.

Is there an unloved and marginalised group that God might be drawing your attention to?

Vision

The core purpose that drives One Eighty lies in its name. We are desperate to see young people turn around from where they are and walk towards God, never looking back. The first word John the Baptist said was 'repent'. Jesus' first sermon began with 'repent'. Repent simply means to turn around, and this is what we are longing to see. In my opinion, there are some balances we must hold correctly in order for this to happen:

1. Youth Ministry not Youth Work – "How can they believe in the one of whom they have not heard? And how can they hear without someone preaching to them?" (Romans 10:14)

Evangelism is all of what we do, it's just what this looks like in practice that changes. I'm not interested in One Eighty the ramp company, or One Eighty the facility provider, or even One Eighty the skate project. I am passionate about One Eighty the evangelistic outreach; reaching relevantly, preaching the word of God and seeing young people connect back to God for the rest of eternity.

I am a professionally qualified youth worker, and I believe in the systems and policies of my practice wholeheartedly. However, I won't let them take a higher place than proclaiming the gospel and, yes, I mean verbally as well as practically and demonstratively. It is so easy for youth ministries to compromise their core mission and end up as little more than a substitute for a secular youth service or organisation. At One Eighty, we are constantly asking ourselves questions: what makes us different? How do people know we're about Jesus? Who and what is the focus of what we do? If it's not God, what's the point?

Is your work obviously and explicitly Christian? Do you think it is essential that everyone knows "we're about Jesus"?

2. Building bridges not islands – "Let us not give up meeting together, as some are in the habit of doing, but let us encourage one another – and all the more as you see the Day approaching" (Hebrews 10:25)

Church is difficult, especially when it comes to feeding young people into the church that have spent their whole lives being disconnected from it. The bible talks about church as God's 'bride'; it's what God loves and is excited about, it's his kingdom here on Earth. But it's run by people, which means it's full of faults and doesn't always provide the right expression of fellowship for the young people we work with. Religion, culture, tradition and rituals can be barriers to young people experiencing God. But church does work and there are churches that are passionate about connecting young people and providing for them.

One thing we are not trying to do is become a youth church, or a separate entity from the church. The church is about the Body of Christ, the family of God. We are a part of the body, but we're not all of it. Therefore, One Eighty is reaching and discipling young people in a way the church is not, and we hope the church is discipling and mentoring these young people in a way we cannot.

I can't give young people in depth teaching from the bible, worship and a room full of hundreds of people who love God and know what it is to experience God. But church can. One Eighty will not exist forever, the church will. If youth ministry is to connect young people to God in a life lasting way, it must not just work with the church, but accept it can't function properly without the church.

The only reason YFC exists is because we need to do the things the church isn't doing. I would love to be out of a job because the church was already reaching these young people, but they're not, so here we are. Part of where One Eighty needs to go is to be taken over and run by the church.

3. Disciples not Converts – "You did not choose me, but I chose you and appointed you to go and bear fruit—fruit that will last" (John 15:16)

A recent outreach event to skaters in this country saw hundreds of young people hear the gospel from a professional skateboarder, and about fifty young people put their hands up to become Christians. Only then was follow up thought about and most of those skaters are not in contact with a Christian now. If follow up preparation had been put in before the event, these young people might now be in church.

Anybody can create converts; all you need is an event or weekend away with lots of 'cool' leaders and an evening meeting involving music and emotional, persuasive communication techniques resulting in an altar call. I'm not saying we shouldn't have altar calls or even persuasive communication techniques but I'm saying this should all be a part of a larger programme and strategy that has been carefully worked out and planned. Jesus didn't just do his thing and leave: from the second his ministry began he trained up a specific group of people to carry on what he had started, he taught people how to pray, encouraged them to meet together, eat together, drink wine together. He never aimed for converts; but he made disciples.

If you create converts, they will create more converts, leaving a flaky church that fall away at the first hurdle. If you create disciples, they will create disciples leaving solid people with solid routes. We don't want young people to be in a relationship with God for a weekend away, a week or a year; we want them to be in a relationship with God for all of eternity.

Is your mission strategy carefully linked to a follow-up and discipleship strategy? If not, what can you do to begin building this part of the process?

4. Faith not Formula – "The righteous will live by faith" (Romans 1:17)

Go into any Christian book shop today and you will find hundreds of books telling you how to be a good leader, how to run a church, how to run a youth ministry, how to live your life. Some of these books can be helpful and educational, but there is a danger we can just copy the methods of someone else because we think that method will work in our situation.

One Eighty gets many requests and enquiries from other organisations trying to set up something similar. They phone the office expecting us to give them some secret code that will unlock the door to their perfect skate ministry. If there is a code, I don't have it!

All I've done is try stuff I've felt God wanted me to do and refuse to give up. If it was rubbish I've tried something else. If it was good, I've kept doing it. That it is the nearest thing I have to a code or formula. People don't go through flow charts, people don't fit in boxes, and therefore ministries that work with people shouldn't either.

Most would agree that we are called to be unique, that we shouldn't compare ourselves to others, that we are all created differently. So if we think this about ourselves, why don't we apply it to our ministries? Don't do something because you've seen it work somewhere else. Be inspired by other ministries, but come up with your own flavour, something that fits the people you work with and the culture you're in.

God is the awesome creator; take a look at our world! He made us to create and to be creative. So don't be boring and copy everyone else, create something that's never been done before. The future of innovative youth work lies in the hands of those who take risks with creative and crazy ideas.

5. Being not Doing – "You have persevered and have

> endured hardships for my name, and have not grown weary. Yet I hold this against you: You have forsaken your first love." (Revelation 2:3-4)

I lied when I said there are no formulas in ministry or life; there is one which I have learnt the hard way. If you neglect your personal relationship with God, everything will fall apart. God doesn't care a tiny bit about your ministry or work compared to how much he cares about you. When Jesus appointed his twelve disciples in Mark 3, the first thing they were called to do, before casting out demons, or healing, was to 'be with him'. Don't fall into the trap of doing instead of being. God wants you, not your work, nor your ideas, not your policies or practice. If you remember nothing from this chapter, remember that.

Theory into Practice

One Eighty owns a mobile skate park which has been in use in Bath and the surrounding areas since January 2004. We have one full time Skate Outreach Manager (that would be me), year out volunteers, youth work students and local volunteers. However, our aim and vision is not just to provide and staff a facility. We hope to "relevantly and contextually proclaim the gospel of Jesus Christ through words, actions and example to young people who are a part of the skate culture and community of Bath".

Weekly Sessions – We hire out a local youth centre to put on a two hour skate session for young people, with volunteers from local churches. This session is very much the 'HQ' of 180, where we feed young people in from other work, and the only session we really make any consistent effort to advertise. The session stops half way through for our 'Think Slot', a short talk given by a staff member. These talks have been on a variety of topics chosen by both staff and young people. They are always interactive, well planned and evangelistic. Simon had been coming to One Eighty for a few months when he said he wanted to be a Christian, after one particular 'Think Slot'. We prayed with him and through our volunteers we were able to integrate him into a local church that he now attends every week.

Thrive – This is our schools enrichment course, designed to help schools meet their extended schools targets in an exciting and relevant way as well as engage with young people who might not excel academically. It is a six week course that can be turned into an after school club. Each week has a different theme. Young people are encouraged to set targets for themselves each week and if they complete all six weeks they receive a certificate. Josh was one young person we came into contact with through a Thrive session in a local school. He had significant behavioural problems and we were informed by a teacher he might not complete the course as he was probably going to be expelled within the next month. Josh was very difficult at first, but after being let loose on the ramps he loved it, and his behaviour during our sessions was, according to one teacher; "the best I've ever seen from Josh". He completed the course.

Detached Work – A crucial part of our work, detached work sees two One Eighty workers heading out to local skate parks and spots to engage with young people where they are, rather than just expecting them to come to us. It also allows us to form relationships with people who don't come to our Tuesday night sessions. Ben was a young person who always came to the skate park after school to hang out with his girlfriend and other friends. We began to chat with him, and after a few weeks a conversation about him wanting to give up cannabis led to us being able to refer him onto a local drugs information service for young people. He thanked us, saying "I don't know who else I would have talked to about that stuff."

Graff – A partnership project with the local council, Graff is a project for young people who are involved in illegal graffiti, or young people who are at risk of being involved in illegal graffiti. Young people can just turn up, or be referred by the police, Youth Offending Team or other youth work professionals. Graff runs at the same time and place as our weekly sessions. Young people sketch and spray paint on boards, then join in with the Think Slot with the skaters. There is a natural link between graffiti and skate culture, so lots of the young people skate and come to Graff. We have also launched 'Graff Connect' for the more committed artists, which is a group funded and staffed by a local church and their arts college[1] as a bridge between the Tuesday night sessions and church. There are many exciting stories from Graff. The culture of graffiti artists mean they rarely engage with youth provision, or even people outside of their 'crews'. They find secluded spots late at night to paint and can spend hours in solitude sketching in their 'black books'. So the fact that a culture completely untouched by the church are engaging with us and hearing about Jesus every week is fantastic.

Is there a particular sub-culture that is linked to the group you work with? Might there be an obvious route for the expansion of your ministry here?

Trips – We hold termly trips to other skate parks around the country. These are great for relationship building and can be an opportunity for young people to gain more confidence by trying higher ramps and bigger obstacles than they would normally.

Events – We can be hired out to hold skate events in the South West, and occasionally beyond, but we keep these to a minimum as there are other great companies who do this.[2]

Switch – Switch is a course written by One Eighty workers designed to introduce skateboarders to the basics of Christianity. This course will be published for others to use in 2008.

Existing Provision – We work with the local skate industry and the council to be a voice for young people in existing skate provision.

Our Weaknesses

Lack of people – It is vital to the ministry of One Eighty that we have committed skateboarders on our team. Finding people who love skateboarding, love God and want to combine the two to reach young people isn't easy. I don't think you have to be a skater to reach skaters, in the same way that you don't have to be a young person to reach young people, but I do believe skaters have it much easier by the way that initial cultural barriers are melted away, speeding the relationship building process up massively.

Young people just need people who will consistently love them, but they do respond better to people who have more in common with them.

Are there any areas of genuinely shared interest and enjoyment that you share with the young people you work with? Could you use these to accelerate the development of relationship?

Encouraging sub culture – Our ministry is based around a specific culture, therefore it is, naturally, seen as endorsing that culture. There are some parts of skate culture I love and that parallel incredibly with biblical principles. However, there are also things about skate culture I can't stand, things that bind up and stifle our young people, stopping them from being the men and women of God they are called to be. Culture-specific ministry endorses the culture it serves – this can be a weakness.

Culture based – Our ministry reaches skaters. Someone who doesn't skate would be welcome to attend but they wouldn't have much to do. Young people can change their culture and interests, meaning we can lose them. When they are done with skateboarding, they are usually done with us. We need to find a way of having a multi faceted ministry that enables young people to drop in and out of different sub cultures, but doesn't allow a loss of contact when they do this.

Is it possible that your work / ministry is too tightly associated with one (possibly short) life-stage, or one particular aspect of the young person's life? What could you do to make your ministry more "multi-faceted"?

Conclusion

One Eighty has been the craziest rollercoaster ride of my entire life. I have sobbed on my knees for skaters to just get a little bit closer to God, I have screamed and shouted at people who just didn't get it, I have shaken with fear, cried with joy, ached with exhaustion. I have loved every second and I am thankful to God for allowing me to even be a part of this incredible ministry, let alone run it and get paid for it.

No book will tell you exactly what you need to do and how you need to do it. That's something you have to figure out. But I can promise you that while you're figuring it out, and doing it, God will never leave you or forsake you; nothing is impossible for him; he will finish the work he has started in you; and he will work for good in all things. He will never let you be tested more than you can stand and NOTHING can separate you from his love.

There is a broken and dying world, which needs restoring and bringing back to life. Find out what makes you angry, check it makes God angry too, and then do something about it together. What are you waiting for?

Notes

1 www.christiancitychurch.eu/bathandbristol for the church and www.cccbathandbristolcolleges.com for the arts college
2 www.tribeskate.com

For further reflection ...

Jo Dolby writes: "I lied when I said there were no formulas in ministry or life; there is one which I have learnt the hard way. If you neglect your personal relationship with God, everything will fall apart. God doesn't care a tiny bit about your ministry or work compared to how much he cares about you."

Do you find it easy believe that God cares more about who you are than about what you do?

Does your personal relationship with God thrive in spite of the pressure and busyness of life and ministry?

What would help you to refresh and re-invigorate your devotional life – a weekend retreat ... a new pattern of daily prayer ... a good book ... time with a spiritual mentor? Will you take that step?

CHAPTER NINE

Sharing the Kingdom

The challenge of mission in an urban setting

Helen Gatenby

"The Gospel teaches us that the bottom line in thinking about discipleship has something to do with staying"[1], asserts Rowan Williams, and my story about our experiences in Manchester explores this link between discipleship and staying. My part in it begins eighteen years ago, when, as an enthusiastic and naïve 21-year-old, I moved into a deck-access maisonette, on an inner-urban housing estate just south of Manchester City Centre to engage in 'incarnational youth work'. I thought I would see God change the world, or at least Brunswick, and expected to see loads of young people come to faith. Well, 18 years later and hopefully a little wiser, Brunswick estate is still my home – having married the vicar, we now live together in the vicarage with our two children – and I continue to work with local young people. And if anything has changed over time, I would say it is me.

Does this sort of length of commitment scare you or inspire you? Why?

My move to Brunswick was in response to what I believed was a clear call from God; to make my home in what many consider is a 'tough and deprived' inner-city housing estate, to be part of the lively Anglican parish church and to work with local young people beyond the usual reach of the church. At the time I had no idea how long I might be here, although within eight months of moving in, God challenged me to a long-term view, asking whether I would be willing to stay 10 years. For someone in their early twenties, this seemed almost beyond what I could imagine, but it is what I sought to commit to, again in a rather naïve way.

After five years of working as part of the local church, it became apparent there was no more money within the church to pay for a youth worker; a reflection of the poor economic status of the parish. I faced a choice; stay, continue working with young people in the area and raise my own finances, or go somewhere else that could pay me. As the second option didn't seem part of God's call, I chose to explore the first. I prayed and talked with people, pushed a few doors and in January 1995, in partnership with local churches and a Youth for Christ ministry in North Manchester, the M13 Youth Project was born, named after the postcode we work within.

The project began with me as an unpaid volunteer. In 1998, it employed both myself and its second worker, Chris Macintosh (who is still with us, as part of his and his family's long-term commitment to the area), and it currently employs six people who spend time on the streets, meeting young people through detached youth work, listening to them and working together with them to develop activities and projects that seek to foster learning, make for human well-being and that enable young people to take action.

When asked about the 'type' of young people we work with, we remember first that young people are our brothers and sisters, fellow human beings, created in the image of God and therefore capable of loving, thinking, creating, achieving and taking action to make a positive difference to their and our world. Young people are often portrayed as other than this; as hoodies, thugs, criminals, economic units, and as 'different to us', as 'objects' to be worked on and changed. We seek to hold young people's humanity as central to our work together.

As walking the streets is our main initial point of contact with young people and where much of our 'work' happens, the young people we work with tend to be local, which means they live within some of the most deprived areas in the country. They have little or no contact with institutional church; they are from diverse ethnic backgrounds, predominantly Black, Asian and white, and most, but not all, will have been born within the UK; they range in age from 13–19, although having been here so long, quite often young adults in their twenties stop by to see us, or seek us out for specific support, and some younger than 13 are keen to work with us, too. All the young people we work with face serious challenges simply through living in the area; Ardwick Ward has one of the highest rates of poor health, child poverty, poor education and low employment. There are serious incidents of drug and gun crime locally; almost everyone will be related to, or know, someone who has been shot, the most recent shootings happening in June and July this summer in the middle of the area we work in, resulting tragically in the loss of two lives and leaving behind parents, partners, children, friends and a community mourning their deaths. Although it sounds sensational, many people have to manage the effects of such violence on a daily basis.

In thinking about what we are trying to achieve, it is probably worth making the distinction between what we hope for (community transformation) and M13's part in working towards that, which, to us, can often seem very little.

We seek to foster learning which makes for human well-being and which enables young people to take action. In essence we work to support change in young people, change that both ennobles and transforms them and their communities, that helps them be fully in touch with their humanity and other's humanity. It is important to recognise that Christ's work with people and communities does not only transform those cultural elements and practices which don't honour him, but it also ennobles those cultural practices which do.

These aims (learning and transformation within young people) are set within the context of our hope to see whole communities transformed and ennobled. We have found it impossible to divorce the issues young people face from the context in which they live. The issues – poverty, poor educational opportunities, few jobs, lack of appropriate resources – are not an individual's 'personal troubles' alone, but the 'public issues' of many young people and of our society as a whole, both across the country and across generations[2]. It would be both foolish and iniquitous of us to ignore the interplay between the personal and the public and how each helps us understand the other. So we hope for 'shalom'[3] within Ardwick and other areas of the city and the country; not simply 'peace', in the sense of the absence of war, fighting or disturbance, as it is most often translated and understood; but justice, right relationships between people, interdependence, wholeness, well-being, health, joy, sufficiency, both personally and communally[4]. This 'macro' vision helps shape the way we think and work with young people, and vice versa.

As each of us joined the project, many of our initial hopes for change were commonly held desires *for* people (often based around economic wealth and a particular kind of 'moral' health) but they were not in many cases appropriate ones, in that they were not shaped by the gospel but *by the only way we had seen the gospel* lived out; ie. within the middle-class culture and church backgrounds from which we had come. We have spent a long time becoming untangled from this and learning how the gospel may be lived out authentically within the culture in which we are based.

To what extent is your understanding of Christianity shaped by your background? Does this negatively limit or affect your work in any way?

So, what do M13 workers do? On one level it's fairly basic: we walk the streets come rain or shine; we spend time with young people we meet there, often on their terms; we are available, we listen, we support and encourage; and we wait and watch attentively to see what happens. When something does, when we notice something or when a young person comes to us with something, we do our best to work with young people through that situation or issue, aiming to foster learning. Some issues or situations are easy, satisfying and fun to work with; others are difficult and push us right to the edge of our comfort zones and beyond.

One such difficult situation was listening to a young man reveal how he had resorted to extreme, pre-emptive violence against another family, because he felt it was the only option available to him to protect his own family, as the police would do nothing until it was too late. Another was listening to two girls re-live the horror of witnessing a street shooting round the corner from their house, of how they had cradled their wounded friend in the middle of the street, trying to keep him alive until the ambulance arrived, struggling to comfort and reassure him in the midst of their own absolute panic. Another was being with a young woman as she faced her fears about her upcoming leg amputation, staying with her in hospital through the night before the operation and beyond. Another was listening to a distraught younger mum recount the pattern of arguing and physical fighting she and her partner just couldn't seem to get out of, some of which happened in front of their young children. And another was sitting with a young man grieving the death of his friend, as he voiced the feelings of many when he said, "Today is shit and tomorrow will be shitter."

It is hard, almost unbearable, to listen to someone you care deeply about telling you how they feel about some of the awful things that have not only happened or are happening to them, but which they themselves have done, both of which diminish their humanity. It is tempting to retreat and natural to want to judge, but we've found it is important to do neither. We've learned to remain there with the young person and remain open to them, holding their humanity as central to our dialogue, so they too can remain in touch with it.

Often careful and loving listening like this is enough to enable a young person to come to their own sound judgements about their actions or their situations. At other times, we find ourselves exploring and challenging what we hear in an attempt to help young people enlarge their view of themselves and the situation for the better.

One night, Jamie, whom we'd known for five years, turned up at Drop-in asking us to write him a character reference for court; he'd been involved in a street robbery, the culmination of some remarkably stupid and bad choices we'd heard he'd been making of late. Rather than just say 'yes' or 'no' to his request, or tell him what we thought about his actions, we saw this as an opportunity to talk with him and maybe help him to think for himself about what he had been doing. When asked what *he hoped we would write* about him compared with what *we actually could write*, Jamie begun to realise that his hopes for himself and his life were a long way from the reality of his recent actions. He glimpsed himself through someone else's eyes and began to think differently. This, along with what was for him the shock of the court process, led him to think and act differently. We were available when he needed us and the trust we had built up over time meant we were able to challenge him in a way he understood and responded to. We hung around and waited and seized the moment when it appeared. Jamie made the changes and actually did the work of transforming his life.

Has your relationship with the young people ever become so cozy and pleasant that you find it hard to challenge them when it is required?

Another opportunity for learning arose when some weights were stolen from the Drop-In venue by a group new to the club. Not an experience we would have chosen to work with, but one that presented itself and that offered us and the guys a chance to explore our common humanity. The following week Chris had a quiet word with one of the guys who would have known what had happened, explaining that the weights belonged to the vicar and were used regularly by the Community Circuit Training group. He suggested that if the weights found their way back to church, we'd be very grateful and that would be the end of the matter. To be honest, we weren't that hopeful (perhaps to our shame), although we weren't going to let the group know that, but we thought it was important to create space for the group to have chance to right their wrong. A couple of weeks later, to our surprise, the weights rolled in – literally – balanced on the handlebars of a bike ridden by one of the group. He handed them to us and we simply said "Thanks, we really appreciate you bringing them back," and that was that. That incident still makes me smile! Not because of the weights themselves, but because of what their return represented – the lads taking a risk in trusting us and choosing to put right something they had done wrong.

Whatever young people bring us, we aim to take it seriously and respond to what they say or want to do. This means we sometimes run the risk of being taken for a ride, but mostly as a result of this approach young people and M13 workers end up working on other positive projects and activities together, like residentials, skills-based workshops, trips and on larger pieces of community action. We try to avoid becoming 'providers' of activities and doing things *for* young people; when asked "Will you organise a trip for us?" we often say "No, we won't..... but we will work together *with* you to help you do it." The theories of Freire[5] and of Informal and Community Education[6] have profoundly influenced the way we think and work. So, we work with *young people's* agenda, together *with* them, (rather than *on* them or *for* them), whilst also having in mind our aim to foster learning within young people, whether through conversation on a detached session on the street, through a five-minute 'incidental chat' during a trip or through an agreed project or programme of 'learning activities' set up together with the young people.

It was suggested to us that a good analogy of our work is that of a golf-caddy, (or to use a biblical picture, that of an armour bearer); walking alongside young people, helping them think and understand their context, choose the right equipment for the task, working together with them to assess the shots they need to make, the lay of the land, any external conditions they need to consider, and then, when the time is right, stepping back and encouraging the young people to find the courage to step up and 'take the shot' themselves, whatever that might be. This way of working has given space for some surprising and encouraging developments within young people.

In summer 2002, we set up some arts workshops, engaging a wide range of young people we met on the streets. In the October, we had a Community Talent Show, where everyone could showcase their talent. The church amphitheatre was packed with community folk but, right up until people actually got on stage to perform, we had no idea whether the performers were even going to turn up. They did, and the event was typically chaotic and fabulous, creating a real buzz! I remember standing at the back of the church, looking at what was happening and thinking; this is where God is, in the chaos with us celebrating the talents of young people.

The following summer, we arranged a meeting with the same young people to discuss what activities they wanted to do that year, expecting the usual suggestions, eg. Alton Towers, etc. The group responded by saying they wanted to do something for the younger ones on the estate, to help them in the way they themselves hadn't been helped and give them the support and advice they needed which they hadn't received. (So much for what we, as M13, hoped we'd been doing!) However, they did want M13 to help them, so we worked together with them on their idea and their agenda, offering basic first-aid and child protection training, and supporting them in planning and running an activity club for 7–11 year olds through the summer. The group who ran the club were aged 13-16, and their work and dedication really began to change the negative view some of the adult residents held about these same teenagers, whom they often saw out on the streets. It also influenced the young people's view of themselves, from young people who joined in with other's activities, to young people who had the capacity, initiative and talent to set up their own activities, to take control and take action which benefited others.

Are you willing to accept and respond appropriately to legitimate criticism?

This was the beginning of the young people taking action on their own initiative to improve their community and the seeds of Community Spirit were born. Two more projects followed over the next two years; a six-week peer-mentoring project and a 5-month weekly youth club for 11–14's, for which, in 2006, the group received the prestigious City Council "Pride of Manchester Award". Since then, this motivation has rippled outward and other young people have asked if we can help them set up their own projects, get involved in peer-mentoring or get involved in youth or children's work.

Coming from an evangelical background, it hasn't always been easy to find a theology for informal education in an urban poor area. Early on, I clearly remember a point where I felt I faced a stark choice theologically, and I'm probably not alone in this. Two or three years into the work, I had seen none of the revival I'd been led to expect would happen when we 'trust God, give our lives and set out to work for him'. Signs and wonders were evident in churches in other more affluent areas of the country, but it wasn't happening here. I asked myself, "Have I got it right theologically, and God just isn't here with the poor and marginalised, as I don't see any evidence of him as I was told I would? Is God here with the poor and marginalised, but I can't yet see it." Either large parts of my faith had to make room for change or I had to give up on God being interested in the poor and leave. But I could not abandon my belief that God loves the poor and so I let go of parts of my theological framework, sought God and stayed. Abba Moses, one of the Desert Fathers, answered a monk who requested a word from him by saying "Go, sit in you cell and your cell will teach you everything,"[7] and as Chris likes to say, for us, Ardwick is our cell; Ardwick has taught us everything and continues to.

Returning to the opening theme of discipleship and staying, Williams continues by exploring the idea of discipleship as one of remaining with Christ, sharing his company. He says of his (and now my) hero Bishop Thomas French, a CMS missionary who worked in the Persian Gulf at a time when there were very few Christians there;

> *He wasn't there first to make converts, he was there first because he wanted to be in the company of Jesus Christ: Jesus Christ reaching out to and seeking to be born in those he worked with.*[8]

When I read this, it moved me deeply and for me it is a reflection of the understanding God has revealed to me of a better motive for being here in Manchester; not that I don't seek young people to know and love Jesus and to be transformed, but that first, it is about keeping company with Jesus. In answering the question, 'Where are we to find Christ?', Williams goes on to extend this idea of keeping Jesus' company, to include being where Jesus is, with the company He Himself keeps. He writes,

> *We are to be not only where he is in terms of mission and outreach and service in the world, where he is in serving the outcast; we are also to be where he is in his closeness to the Father. We follow him, not simply to the ends of the earth, to do his work and echo his service; we follow him to be next to the heart of the Father.*[9]

This two-fold manifesto, of being with Jesus in place (serving the outcast) and in spirit (being next to the Father's heart) describes our journey, going deeper into a place and a faith which is less driven by activity and more shaped by contemplation and love of our heavenly Father and of the people we live with[10].

What stories and testimonies from the past or the present challenge and inspire you?

So, over time, as we have worked and learned, we have become less driven by the need to be 'doing' things for people and more interested in being with, in contemplating and then in acting out of our contemplation with people. Our journey has been both beyond ourselves, stretching our comfort zones, learning to live with what we thought we couldn't, and seeking to find God where we thought He wasn't. But it has also been a journey into ourselves, to seek and find God, the love of God within us for ourselves and others, and to learn the true meaning of Love. We remain with a people who live, often with great love and dignity, within both terrible and joyful situations and it is our privilege to share our lives together. And we continue to have hope[11] and to try and learn to make God-sense of what happens here together with young people. "And" to (slightly mis-) quote Stewart Henderson "while we may yearn for that faultless city many of us continue to [abide] in imperfect settlements [with imperfect people], which often remind us, in the strangest of ways, of that which is to come."[12]

Notes

1 Williams, R. (2007) Being Disciples. http:// www.archbishopofcanterbury.org/sermons_speeches/070427.htm

2 Wright Mills, C (1970) The Sociological Imagination. London: Penguin

3 Jeremiah 29:4-7, especially verse 7

4 Punton, J (1975) The Community of Shalom; God's Radical Alternative. FYT. http://johndavies.org/jimpunton-shalom.pdf

5 Freire, P. (1972) Pedagogy of the Oppressed. London: Penguin

6 see Deer Richardson, L. & Wolfe, M. (eds) (2001) Principles and Practices of Informal Education; Learning Through Life. Abingdon: RoutledgeFalmer

and also the YMCA George Williams College "Informal and Community Education" DipHE course.

7 Ward, B. (1975) The Sayings of the Desert Fathers. Michigan: Cistercian Publications

8 Williams, as above

9 Williams, as above

10 echoing Psalm 27:8

11 Psalm 27:13-14

12 Henderson, S. (2000) Urban Angel; Exploring the Soul of the City. Carlisle: Piquant & Alpha

For further reflection ...

Helen Gatenby has been working in Brunswick for eighteen years! And she recognises that, perhaps, it is her and her understanding of God and his purposes in mission that have changed more than anything around her. She writes, "I could not abandon my belief that God loves the poor and so my faith began to change."

Have your views and understandings been changed by your time working with young people?

Are you willing to face hard questions with the same bravery that Helen showed and to see your faith and your style of ministry change as a result? Who can help you to work through these issues?

What are the particular questions that you struggle with? What effects might fresh answers to these questions have on the way you go about your life and work?

CHAPTER TEN

The House that Jack Built

Mission and inclusion in a family

Tim Evans

'Council estate ministry is the new Africa,' said a friend, recently. What he meant was that people who decided to live on council estates were being portrayed by some as the new heroes of Christian mission – going to places of deepest darkness, exoticness and danger to bring our white middle class light! What is worse is that some fall into the temptation of believing the hype and enter into a kind of tussle for whose estate is the roughest, hardest, most dangerous ensues. So it is with some trepidation that I tell you my wife and I live on an estate in Birmingham with our four foster children. In my day job I work for a small national Christian charity, Worth Unlimited which works with young people on the margins of society. This is the story of my working life. I have been passionate about those who find themselves on the back end of society and ignored and despised by the church ever since, as a new Christian, I foolishly volunteered for a detached youth work project at University. This does not make me a hero, just tired... and often wondering why on earth I continue to attempt to believe in those who find it so hard to believe in themselves.

Sometimes we feel like 'heroes'; more often we're "just tired". How do you think God views you? How do you think he would have you view yourself?

I don't want to tell you about my organisation – go to www.worthunlimited.co.uk for that! Instead, I would like to tell you about a little project that my wife Ria and I have started as a new way of engaging and supporting vulnerable young people. I hope you forgive me but some history as to how we have arrived where we are is required. You do not have to work with these young people for very long or live in their communities for five minutes to discover that, whilst the professional world would like them to have issues and crises between the hours of 9 to 5 and will provide funding only for a 10 week course to sort them out, unfortunately their often chaotic lives do not fit so neatly! So we, like many others, have had young people live with us, which is why we decided to begin fostering. We have young people in and out of the house – and hanging round the front. (Currently, this is due, at least in part, to a group of young lads taking a shine to one of our foster daughters!)

I have worked for a YMCA and Ria has been doing some counselling for a young person's homeless charity, so we have seen hostel or direct access housing at first hand. (Indeed, we lived in a YMCA for two years to prove the point!) We've also had young people around us, living with us and even being fostered by us, then watched them return to hostels or council flats. Frustrated, we sat down one night and started to chat about what would *really* make a difference to these young people at vulnerable stages of their lives. We came up with a rather surprising conclusion: family! These were young people at vulnerable transition times in their lives – leaving prison, leaving care, leaving or being kicked out of home. For some these other environments worked fine for them and they would make positive transitions into new phases of their lives. But this was the key – they were especially vulnerable at these transition times and, if we could do something about it, we could potentially prevent them sliding (further) into crime, drugs, homelessness, benefits dependency, unwanted pregnancy – in fact all the things that the government spends billions of pounds tackling every year. Many of these young people needed to be engaged with the more informal support mechanisms of that a family provides. A family would allow them to learn skills for life, like budgeting and cooking. It would also encourage them to develop character skills – self-esteem, confidence, perseverance and aspirations – for a better life by experiencing it. Replacing the ten week course would be learning to live life in all its rawness and fullness with others trying to live life in a meaningful way. It would not mean we did not want 'professional' input into their lives but that the focus of trying to hold their lives together would be something more permanent – something they often lacked from adults.

Is there any way that you could begin to harness the power of 'family' in your work and ministry?

These reflections were partly a result of our reflecting on what happened to Jack (not his real name) who had lived with us for six months after being discharged originally from a hostel and then from a police station. He had many issues but whilst with us made good progress including deciding to become a Christian at a local church. Unfortunately, despite describing themselves as an inner city church they did not have a clue as to how to deal with someone who had anger and drug issues, deep seated pastoral issues that needed to be worked through. Their view: surely all he needed was Jesus and everything would be alright? In the meantime we did not have the time to support him as much as we would have liked and so he came to a point of us moving him on to a supported flat. However, the support was not very well thought through and finished around 4pm – about two hours after Jack often got up. He slipped back into his drug taking, got kicked out of the flat, and stopped attending church. We have not heard from him for a couple of years now.

What was clear was that we needed a project – housing, mentoring and either meaningful work or training – that combined informal and professional support for the Jacks of this world.

I know many people who open up their homes to young people,

some offering substantial opportunities for young people living with them. I am often asked for advice as to how young people, often difficult, troubled and chaotic, can work within family life. The truth is that it is not easy. Jane (not her real name) came to stay in the project with us. Her childhood had been taken from her through abuse and she had no sense of self, who she was and what she was worth. She wanted to be older than she was but acted a lot younger. It felt as if we were managing her, trying to help her avoid the inevitable consequences of her behaviour – consequences that could severely affect the rest of her life. However hard we tried, she did not form attachments but robbed, ran away, hung out with much older men and in the end just left, deciding she could not cope. Interestingly for us, as painful as the episode was, she seemed unable to respond to the fact that she was not being offered just a 'service' as she had experienced from so many other professionals, but a home and care and a sense of the on-going building block of family life.

Ann (not her real name) was completely different. Theories around attachment have really helped us understand the tentative steps young people, battered by life and behaviourally responding, need to take to believe that they can let go a little, trust a little, communicate a little, care a little and be cared for in return. Ann came to us, shy, reserved. We let her settle and tried to give constant messages that we were there for her; that we were not going to abandon her as she had experienced from others. We tried to be consistent in our dealings with her, always explaining our reasoning and trying to encourage her to make positive choices herself. She gradually opened up and was able to share some of her experiences. Mainly though, she was able to lift her head up. By believing in herself a little more she was able to do things a little more. She enjoys our church community who are all supportive, if not completely understanding, of her and she values that. She is coming to understand that if we stood by her and were there for her then perhaps the same can be said for God.

The project involves purchasing property – a four bedroomed

house on a buy-to-let mortgage and we have put in an offer for another. One of these properties is situated next door to us, making the support process much easier. The young people are referred by an agency or worker, someone who has engaged with them in whatever context and feels this project will meet needs identified. We then interview the young people and if suitable talk them through the welcome pack that outlines what living in the house involves. We assign them a mentor, who begins to work with them on an action plan. This can include little things such as communicating with others in the house or larger things like jobs or training. The project aims to be self sustaining. Once we have two houses we anticipate that housing benefit or rent will pay for the employment of at least a worker part-time to help manage the project and provide mentoring and support to these young people. Even the whole aspect of filling in housing benefit forms is very time consuming. We also have to think of maintenance and breakages, for rooms sometimes being empty and budget for all of these. Housing provides the stable context for engaging often chaotic young people – it becomes a place where they experience some stability and therefore can begin to think and act in a more stable fashion. This then enables the engagement with other issues in their lives which are often deep rooted and complex. Much housing provision makes the mistake of either providing very little support or support that is so intense that the young person feels suffocated. By befriending we aim to give a sense of relational security alongside the physical security of housing. We hope that over time this will give them the confidence and the stable bedrock to engage in some of the other more challenging areas of their lives.

How does this work on a day to day basis? Young people will often pop round for a chat or for us to try and resolve some conflict in the house. Sometimes they will need to chat for a long time, which can be draining, but you recognise you might be the only person that has ever really listened to them. If we have not seen them for a while then we will pop round to see how things are going. One of the houses is deliberately next door to our house with a joint garden and so naturally we have conversations as they come out into the garden for a smoke. Once a week their mentor comes round to see the young people, chat through both how they are doing in the house and to work with them on their action plan. Often we spend time chatting to the young people about life together and using that to help them think about skills and strategies for life in its widest sense. It is very relational and conversational but underpinning all this is awareness on our part about a) what is really going on for the young person and b) skills, awareness, character issues that we are seeking to work on with them. The other aspect that works really well is fostering younger children. There is something about younger children that engenders an increased sense of responsibility amongst older young people. We also have just started creative groups, which give opportunity for emotional and spiritual reflection. Most of the young people pop into these which are deliberately short sessions.

There have been some young people we have had to ask to leave and one who was rearrested by the police. There is also a gender difference around ability to communicate and reflect and how individuals are influenced by their peers. This has meant, for the boys, trips to football, etc., where we can chat more informally over an activity, whilst the girls are better at just popping round and sitting chatting in the kitchen.

In terms of the values that drive the project we have utilised some of the aims, ethos and theology of Worth Unlimited.

We aim:

- To empower socially excluded young people to move from dependence through independence to interdependence, enabling them to become responsible citizens through positive life style and transformation.

- To provide challenging and creative experiences which

help develop their awareness of spiritual, social, emotional, mental, economic and physical aspects of life enabling them to become contributing members of the community.

Spiritual development has been perhaps the hardest to get our heads around. Our project is underpinned by the biblical understanding of shalom, God's concern for wholeness in both individual and corporate life.

In your ministry do you seek to help young people develop in all the different facets of their lives or do you focus on just one or two? What are the strengths and weaknesses of each approach?

Shalom must always be active; it is a noun that is shaped from a verb. It has in-built energy to work hard in establishing and achieving its goals; "Seek *shalom* and pursue it" (Psalm 34:14) is an essential expectation. *Shalom* is also holistic in the truest sense of the word. It is only truly present when it is active and engaged in bringing about radical change in three overlapping areas of people's lives: well-being, justice and integrity.

- **Well-being.** All material needs must be met: *shalom* means that everyone has enough food to eat, clothes to wear, physical health, a home to live in, a job to be able to provide for themselves and others; everything that makes for wholesome human life – a strong sense of personal fulfilment, a feeling of security and have a deep sense of dignity. Young people must have sufficient, succeed and be safe; want and failure are not *shalom*. Many struggle on the edge of society; they lack personal, social and life skills. They feel excluded from education and training and so regular work becomes increasingly remote. For the most marginalised and socially excluded young people in our society their only real choice seems to be crime, drug pushing or prostitution in order to gain some financial independence. *Shalom* requires that we strive to meet these needs.

- **Justice.** All relationships must be right and just: *shalom* means there must be social justice, positive human relationships as they should be – personal, local or global. The biblical understanding of 'justice' is the process 'to put everything right'. Many young people's already difficult circumstances are exacerbated by a breakdown in relationships at many levels; with their families, authorities and therefore society in general and sometimes even among their peers. This not only fractures communication, and the ability to build and grow essential relationships, but it also creates deep wells of anger, resentment and even hate. They feel like victims or misfits – them against the world. Trapped within a web of real or perceived injustice they fail to thrive. Motivated by this *shalom* demand we work to 'put things right'.

- **Integrity.** All people must have integrity in character: *shalom* means that each person is upright and truthful, dependable, honest and just. They display the moral and spiritual qualities of wisdom and maturity. Young people, who find themselves left behind or left out in our society, frequently develop the negative self-image that anyone on the margins of their own communities develops about themselves. This is only reinforced and amplified by the seeming success story of other young achievers around them. This low self-esteem fragments them emotionally and spiritually and affects their sense of self worth and the desire to make the most out of life. It damages their core integrity. Inspired by this *shalom* imperative we work to make a significant contribution in changing this, helping young people to transform their view of themselves and enabling them to make a valued contribution to their wider world.

The *Shalom* of God's Kingdom is most fully expressed in and experienced through the life, teaching, death and rising again of

Jesus Messiah (the Christ). He is the 'Prince of *Shalom*' and of His *Shalom* there will be no end (Isaiah 9:6-7). His self sacrificial dying was for our *shalom* (Isaiah 53:5), making possible reconciliation with God and of all fractured relationships. Jesus has made "*shalom* through the blood shed on the cross." (Colossians 1:20). He Himself is our *shalom* (Ephesians 2:14). The Good News of *Shalom* is through Jesus Christ who is Lord of all (Acts 10:36). Through Jesus, God makes possible liberation from all that destroys *shalom* in the lives of individuals, families, communities, people and nature. This totally transforming experience of *shalom* is on offer through trusting in Him. To those whose broken lives were restored Jesus said "your trust has made you whole. Go into *shalom*" (Luke 7:50). Our project exists to enable broken and flawed young people to experience God's transforming *shalom* in Jesus Messiah for themselves.

Shalom is fundamentally about hope. It clearly declares not only how things should be but also how they shall be. Young people on the margins of society today often have little hope and much despair. The *shalom* vision is there to inspire us that things can be different and to energise us as we work to make that a reality in their lives.

What hopes and dreams keep you going when things are tough? What can you do to sustain and nourish the hope that is within you?

We have still not worked out the issue of church with these young people – to be honest trying to work with them to hold their lives together takes up enough time as it is! Creative groups, alongside eating together, is our first attempt at exploring this aspect of their lives. There is a growing body of evidence that spirituality is a foundation for resilience, a sense of purpose, and concern for the well-being of others. In our mind it links to notions of fresh expressions of urban church as being pioneered by people such as the Urban Expression network. This involves having others live in urban communities in a self sustaining way able to develop church, support vulnerable people and incarnate the way of Christ. If we had others with us committed to this way of living out being followers of Jesus then I think developing a community of faith would be a more feasible prospect. We currently are part of something called Peace (Shalom) Church in Birmingham, (www.peacechurch.org.uk) based on Ananaptist notions of peace, justice, simplicity and living out being a follower of Jesus in a humble non-authoritarian way, committed to those on the underside of society. However, even this is not localised or contextualised enough for the young people we currently work with and know.

How do the young people you work with relate to local churches in your area?

If I was to dream a little it would be that there would be a few radical followers who would commit to live with us for the next ten years on the estate. We would live simply, share resources and build a common community life together. People would be involved in various aspects of the life of the estate; school, youth work, community groups, local politics, local services building relationships of trust and respect with people, but in particular would support young people in the housing project and seek to draw them into this common life. As I have got a bit older I have learnt to appreciate a more ritualised and contemplative approach to spirituality where space is created for creative reflection, prayer, exploration and dialogue. Our other work with young people has often involved so called 'alternative worship' and non book ways of thinking about our own stories and the narrative of God's story of redemption. In the midst of busy lives and a busy project this becomes actually more necessary for us but also for those we serve where we become 'more than' just a community or housing project, and we do it is a way that engages with the real rawness and down to earth reality of all of our lives. Eating, laughing, crying, going away – these become features of our lives together whilst at the same time not becoming an over intense community that drives away those who do not get their energy from being around people all the time.

Much as I would like to claim that all of the above was thought out in a logical, objective way, I am afraid that at times it hasn't neen and we are still learning. For one we need to put the project on a better footing governance wise. But for good or ill it is in the DNA of how I see faith and how I should be in the world. If we thought about the consequences of trying to bring salvation in its fullest and holistic form to the world I don't think we would ever start. Will we still be going in ten years time? I hope so. But if I have learnt anything it is that if we ourselves are to experience salvation – deliverance from all that dehumanises us, we must recognise that we are our brother's keeper, that we cannot walk by on the other side when we see need. This doesn't mean being naïve or gung ho – there are plenty of young people for which our project is not set up to support and we have needed to try and think out carefully what we are doing and what we have the capacity, skills and resources to do. But it does mean taking a risk, giving it a go, building support around you. This may be out of context but Sherlock Holmes said that when all that is impossible has been eliminated, whatever is left, however implausible, must be reality. We could not see an alternative for some of these young people and so however mad our little scheme seems, that is what we must do.

For further reflection ...

Tim Evans speaks passionately of a vision for work with young people that is based around the biblical concept of *shalom*. "Our project is underpinned by the biblical understanding of *shalom*, God's concern for wholeness in both individual and corporate life."

Do you and/or your church have a clear idea of the vision that underpins all of the varied work that you do?

Could you explain this overall vision clearly and concisely to a member of the public or, more importantly, to potential co-workers?

If you don't have a clear vision of what your work is about, would it be possible to set aside time to work with those in authority over you and with your team to work on such a vision?

CHAPTER ELEVEN

Urban Nites

Sub-urban and spiritual youth ministry

Richard James

Rushing to the Margins

> *"All Tom Hanks wanted was a typical vacation at home." or so starts the YouTube trailer to the 1980s classic film "The Burbs".*

In this smart suburban tale of Suburban discovery Hanks plays Ray Peterson, a regular guy living in a regular area living the regular suburban lifestyle with its weekly commutes to work and weekend care of the house and garden. His life is a pattern that repeats itself year on year and nothing changes, that is until one week when he takes time out from work to lounge around at home and comes to see that strange things are happening at night and the lives of people around him are not as regular as he first thought. Supported by his friend Dern, Peterson engages in an adventure inspired by the bizarre neighbours and discovers more about himself along the way than he does about them.

Like Peterson the area in which I now live and work is a nice suburban area in South West London. Here people live in nice houses, live nice regular lives, engaging in the weekly commute to work and the weekend care of house and gardens. We may have pockets of deprivation, but overall people are reasonably affluent; most need nothing although all want for something. However, should you, like Peterson, take a vacation at home, you would discover that at night this lovely suburban area is not as it first seems and strange things are happening at night.

How might you step outside of your normal ministry routine to get a fresh perspective on what is going on around you?

For me, my tale of the Burbs began in late 2005 when a group of us from Oxygen, Kingston YFC, the youthwork charity I am involved with, took such a vacation from the regular pattern of life and ventured into the night time to see what was going on. Our journey had been brought about by conversations with local residents who had approached us to do something about the problem of young people who were hanging around on the grass outside one of the nice suburban churches late into the evenings. As far as many residents were concerned, these young people were a nuisance: they were drinking considerable amounts of alcohol, smoking cannabis, smashing windows, intimidating people and leaving piles of litter and broken benches when they left.

Various groups had tried responding to this nuisance problem. The council had been in and removed the benches to try and break up the groups that gathered, but this had failed as they had ended up sitting on the kerb or in residents' gardens. Then the police had been drafted in, whose response was to insist that the young people move on and vacate the area. This too had failed, as inevitably each of the groups that had been moved on ended up being directed into the same area, resulting in large gatherings of young people in the town centre and bringing even greater issues.

So as the police and council pondered what to do next, it was Oxygen's chance to wonder about what our response should be. Like all good Christians, we held a meeting, but our meeting was not in a church but over a cup of McDonalds Hot Chocolate just down the road from where the young people were congregating.

Our first idea was to start a new youth club: after all we'd read in papers and many reports about young people that all they wanted was somewhere to go, somewhere to call their own. With this in mind we talked through the options of setting up a new youth club, or even a football project or a music workshop. However despite the appeal of these options, we soon realised that none of them felt right. So we pressed on, exploring options and testing ideas, none of which appealed. It wasn't long before our Hot Chocolate came to an end, and with it our planning meeting, and so in a burst of spiritual energy we decided to pray whilst walking past the group of young people whom we had been talking about, and see what they were up to.

Where do your most fruitful thinking and planning meetings take place? Are you able to include prayer on the agenda?

It was only as we approached that we started to collectively have the obvious idea of how we should respond to this anti social problem – if these young people were being classified as anti social, why not just be social and talk to them? After all the response of two statutory agencies had been anti social in nature – where young people gathered together they had removed the benches so they couldn't meet up, where they had found a place to be social they had moved them on so that they didn't have a chance to find a place to belong. Maybe the best response to anti social behaviour was to demonstrate social behaviour. Where someone has been brought up in an antisocial environment, surely they don't need more of the same; what they need is the opposite.

So, in late 2005 in a lovely Suburban area of South West London a group of volunteers fuelled by a mix of fear and courage approached a group of "anti social" young people and, just as in the life of Tom Hanks in the Burbs, nothing was quite the same ever again!

Urban Nites is born

Our approach to those young people on that first evening soon became our pattern for subsequent weeks. We as workers would meet, chat briefly, pray and then go out to the group of young people. We would go with no particular agenda, we would not try to 'convert' them, nor even generate specific conversations about God; instead we would go and be social because our faith meant we had to. As the nights got colder, so we started taking out hot chocolate in flasks, and packets of biscuits. Soon people in the church next to where we were meeting caught onto what we doing and then we had people offering to pray and make cakes for us to take out.

Local churches aren't always so quick to respond positively to new youth initiatives; what can be done to make a positive response as likely as possible?

Weeks went on, and despite the cold and often small numbers of young people, we persisted, always being in the same place at the same time week after week – the same group of volunteers, offering free hot chocolate, but also someone to talk to or just listen. Eventually word got around and people realised we were 'safe' and so, barring the occasional blip, usually due to a local house party or hail storm we were now regularly attracting up to 30 young people each Thursday night.

Now several years from those initial conversations in McDonalds this project, that has become known to us as Urban Nites, has widened to other areas and deepened in its spiritual input. We have made many mistakes along the way, tried things that haven't worked, come away some nights questioning the validity of it all, or worse with bills for broken windows from footballs kicked by volunteers!

Having revealed some of our heart motivation in stepping out into the night time, I would like to share some of the head practicalities of what we have learnt, often the hard way. Hopefully by revealing some of the unspectacular workings of what have done, we can reveal to you some of the spectacular things that God has done along the way on suburban street corners

What is Urban Nites?

Urban Nites's pattern of practice has become simple. Each week at the same time a team of regular and occasional volunteers meet for prayer before heading out, often with hot chocolate, juice and cakes made by other people in the church. They intentionally go to the places where young people are already gathering, whether this be local estates, town centre shopping areas or just outside in the church graveyard. By going out they leave all the securities that running a club in a building brings with it, but by doing this with offerings of cakes and snacks made by people in the church they take the value of generosity with them.

Where is your safety-zone? What fresh things might you be able to achieve if you were willing and able to leave it behind?

When they arrive this volunteer team meet the young people who regularly congregate in that area. Over time the relationships build and the young people are often found sitting, waiting for the team's arrival and the accompanying chocolate and cakes. Then, unlike a detached youthwork team that would make contact with a group and move on, or an outreach team that seeks out young people to promote a club running somewhere else, the Urban Nites group of volunteers seek to work with that group of young people in that place at that time. There is no desire to use the contact to invite them back to a youth club, or to pass on the necessary information before moving onto to the next 'at risk' group. Instead, over weeks, months and eventually years this team meet with those young people and seek to discover Jesus in the midst of their group through discussions and the introduction of Deepening Activities.

Deepening Activities are planned things that are used to either stimulate conversation or to engage a young person in exploring and experiencing an issue. In the past this has included making and decorating Crucifixes, compiling a God Graffiti (prayer) wall as well as making Solidarity Freedom (Stop the Traffik) bracelets.

Over time, and only after we had gone about establishing relationships in the early stages, we have found that Deepening Activities have given the Urban Nites sessions a direction and conversation triggers. Introducing Deepening Activities too early, we found that these often become the focus of the evening, rather than the young people themselves.

Alongside the Deepening Activities and towards the end of the session a prayer book is also used. This prayer book, a simple A4 hardback notebook, is a vital part of Urban Nites. In the initial weeks and months it is a means by which workers can record things that the young people have shared (not in confidence) to pray for. As the weeks progress so then the book is brought out into the session and the search for prayer requests made explicit. From here it is not long before the young people are taking on the gathering of the prayer requests themselves, asking each other how their various family members, home situations and court cases are going so that they can be prayed for.

Every so often a prayer request will come in that provides us as workers with a unique challenge. On one occasion as the prayer book was gathered and considered, one girl asked if we pray that her boyfriend would die a horrible death. Not wanting to dismiss this out of hand as a mere provocative distraction from what our Evangelical heritage had taught us to be acceptable items for prayer, we sought her out and asked her the reasons for this unusual request. As we drew to one side, we soon realised that this was a girl that was hurting. We already knew she lived in the midst of a terribly broken family environment, but now she revealed how the one person who she had trusted, her boyfriend, had gone behind her back and cheated on her with her best friend. Now any residual trust she had held had all but been destroyed and in an act of anger, born of deep hurt she had wanted compensation. That evening, our prayers took on a new dimension as we prayed not just for her pain, but for her family and for God to place people around her so she could rebuild trust.

Is there a procedure in place in your work for young people to make personal prayer requests known?

There is no greater honour than standing on a street corner, or in the middle of an estate, as prayer requests are shared and a murmured amen is issued by an odd collection of hood covered teenagers. These are young people, who, given the individualism that society inculturates, do not experience environments where people ask them to share how they feel and then care about what they say. Yet on these night time suburban streets we, as Urban Nites workers, have a chance to be a representation of a Loving Father God who wants to hear from us and cares deeply about what we say. So it is that our prayer times become more than a simple end of session God slot, but a time when these young people learn to trust and be honest not only with us, but with a God who cares about the deep hurts in their lives.

However as this pattern of going, chatting, deepening and praying has repeated itself and a regular group of young people has become established, the constant pressure (to which we have occasionally succumbed) is to move the work indoors, to become a regular youth club. Although recently on occasions this has worked, in the early days when we moved inside either on the insistence of the young people or, more often, the volunteers we found the emphasis, and even the theological identity of our work changing.

Working outside allows a person to engage informally in an open environment where we are not distracted into building maintenance or preventing equipment being stolen. As soon as we move inside, staff become split: some are responsible for equipment, some for chatting to young people, others for watching and monitoring behaviour. Young people who would otherwise be in an environment where there were little or no rules, were now in a building where expectations changed. In the outdoors all were equal, chatting and sharing together. Once indoors roles changed, we became rule implementers and they potential rule breakers.

It now seems obvious what was happening but at the time it still took us a while (along with five stolen extinguishers, three broken windows and a lot less fun) to realise what had happened in moving indoors. Then despite the cold and dark we took the decision to move back outside to try and recover some of the ground that we may had lost.

Have you taken time to consider how the location of your work affects the power dynamics and the nature of the relationship between you and the young people? What can be done to improve the situation?

This strange mix of going outside but staying in one place has resulted in a unique mix of work that combines the principles of both outreach and detached work. Like detached work we are separated from a building, but like outreach work we have one place for people to come to. As time has gone on this planting of work in the outside has brought fresh challenges to think about what it means to be Church. As groups have got used to the ritual of talking, deepening and praying so we have been able to explore more matters of faith and life with them, launching Going Deeper groups on other nights. We have also seen the rise of the Urban Nites missionary as some people who come to one scheme help start it in other areas with other young people.

This is youthwork and mission on the margins, both literally and metaphorically. It takes us to the boundaries of the society in which we live and whilst we are there it shows us what it means to follow a God of compassionate love as revealed throughout the Bible.

A God who rushes to the Boundaries

In Luke Chapter 15 Jesus tells a well-known story of a Prodigal Father who rushed to the boundaries to embrace a non-penitent, but hungry son. In telling this parable, he is revealing the heart of a God who himself rushes to the boundaries to embrace the marginalised, joyously celebrating with those are being found there. This is what is happening in Urban Nites. As we move to the boundaries we are seeing people, who out of deep sense hunger are coming. Despite the cakes we offer, their hunger is not physical but rather is for relationship and a sense of meaning. So as we meet these returning prodigals we need to follow the Father in not demanding acts of penitence, or confessions of guilt, but rather being like the servant and joining in the preparations of a celebration, as what was once lost is now being found.

The end of this envisioning parable however warns us that not everyone will understand or want to join with our celebrations. As we know the reaction of the Elder Son was to criticize the Father, rightly pointing out that he had been faithful, done all that was required of him and sacrificed much following his brother's self-centred departure. For us, as Urban Nites workers, rushing to the boundaries opens us up to criticism; people may rightly question our sanity and the justice of spending so much time and possibly money looking to and hoping for those who seem least deserving. But here too in the parable we once again find evidence of the Father's compassion as he once again goes to the boundaries to meet the elder son returning from his work in the field, putting an arm around him and explaining the significance of the celebrations underway. For us, our tension will be maintaining the boundary relationship between the one that returns and the one that threatens to leave. It would be easy to join in the party and exclude and count as out of touch those that in the church have been faithful and kept going year on year. Instead we must once again follow the Father God's example in explaining the significance of the celebrations underway.

Conclusion

As I close my short Suburban tale of Urban Nites I do so with a hope that you too will be inspired by the different way in which we have come to see our neighbourhood. For us the journey of the last few years has been exciting and challenging, one where we have learnt so much about ourselves along the way.

We are now at a point where we are asking questions and trying to work out answers as to what it means to have a church of prodigals. This is alongside the fact that due to the impact that the project is having we have also seen the number of places in which we are being asked to run and train people to run an Urban Nites Project grow.

Given the revelation of the motivation of the compassionate Father God as seen in Luke 15, my hope is that this simple pattern of going, chatting, deepening and praying is not the exception but rather the expectation, that together we can come to see all our neighbourhoods in different ways and in so doing find ourselves constantly celebrating that which was lost being found and what was once dead being alive.

For further reflection ...

Richard James is honest enough to give us an insight into the way that a project like Urban Nites develops ... not in a nice, neat, linear style but with stops and starts, successes and failures. Timing is essential, as is the willingness to recognise mistakes and rectify them.

Do you have processes for the regular evaluation and assessment of your work in place?

Are you and the rest of the team flexible enough to respond appropriately and quickly to the results of these evaluations?

Do you have people that you can discuss progress with and receive advice from?

What would you need to do to make your work more flexible and able to develop?

CHAPTER TWELVE

Schools, Churches – Anywhere we can go!

The Story of XPL, South-East London

Patrick Reagan

'Billy the Kid' was one of the most badly behaved boys in his school. He spent most of his academic life either sitting outside the headmaster's office or in detention as he was constantly in fights with his classmates. He had no self control and, when angry, would often shout and swear at his teachers and would become violent without much provocation. He found it hard to concentrate on his studies and was far from reaching his academic potential. Billy was not a well-liked member of the school.

It would be easy to write Billy off as an aggressive and insolent child. In reality, though, he was a victim. He had been bullied since he started school and his home life was far from perfect. His parents would fight so frequently that he was often afraid to go home.

I was lucky enough to see Billy's life turn around. He started attending XLP's lunchtime club, which I was running in his school. It was by no means a miraculous overnight change but over time his behaviour improved and his self-confidence grew. He began to apply himself at school and eventually achieved much more than any of his teachers thought possible. In fact he is now such an accomplished young man that I invited him to be a guest speaker at XLP's annual meeting.

When times are hard do you have the privilege of being able to look back and think of at least one young person whose life has been turned around? Or has all of your work been in the sowing stage?

As a youth worker seeing someone's life completely turn around is a massive privilege in a calling where it sometimes feels like we are just chucking out mustard seeds. We don't always see how they grow or even get appreciation for playing our part but when we come before God we do have the reassurance that we're growing his kingdom. The story of XLP is about God giving us a passion to see our communities transformed and to see those who have been written off by society going on to lead 'normal' lives, i.e. not going to prison, not getting pregnant in their teenage years and not dying young because they got mixed up in violent gangs. We want the young people to be able to gain qualifications and get a job rather than resort to crime because they think they have no options.

What are the passions that God has given you and that he wants you to use to build the Kingdom?

XLP's roots stretch back to 1994 when I was the 21-year-old youth worker at Christchurch Gyspy Hill. The vicar of my church got a phone call from a secondary school in West Dulwich. There had been a stabbing in the playground and the school was at a loss as to how to deal with the increase in violence amongst its pupils, and was worried about their moral upbringing. They wanted someone to come and speak to the kids and as the youth worker it made sense for me to do it, plus I was well up for it, excited by the challenge it represented. Little did I know, at that stage, just what would emerge as a result of this opportunity. After a lot of thought about what to do for a first lesson I decided it would be good to look at heroes and role models. I'd be working for a while on a local estate, and noticed that the kids were always looking for someone to look up to and so often their dads weren't around to provide a natural role model. For the guys in particular, this was a big issue as they would then look around for someone else to admire. Inevitably it would end up being the bloke who was a few years older than them who was earning hundreds of pounds each week through drugs and other crime and had earned the respect and fear of those around him. If your role model tells you there's no point going to school since you can earn more money illegally than you can spending years striving, then you can imagine what that does to your attitude to studying.

My first class was a group of 15- to 16-year-olds. At 21, I wasn't that much older than they were but the school felt a million miles from the one I'd been in. We'd spent hours at lunchtimes in the playing fields, getting all our energy and aggression out over a game of football, whereas here there was just a small concrete playground and nowhere else to go, even for PE lessons. I soon found myself in a small classroom standing in front of 30 kids who were all going completely mental. I just couldn't believe how riotous it was – the teacher was shouting but the kids were just ignoring him and it took him a full 15 minutes just to get everyone settled down so that I could start. It was pretty intimidating but thankfully they all loved talking about who they looked up to and why and so got pretty involved in the lesson. Over a few years I got the chance to teach every pupil in the school, trying to help them grapple with issues of morality, self confidence and respect.

It was great getting into the classrooms and the kids and teachers were loving the classes but I felt like I needed to be in the schools more so I could get to know some of the young people better. I wanted to have a greater impact and do something less formal so thought that a lunch club might be a good way to start. I felt that to be able to cope with the things life threw at them the young people needed a sense of belonging and a sense of value so these were the things I wanted to work on and improve. Despite the kids enjoying the lessons I'd done, I knew as a Christian there would be an inherited label for the club as being quiet and a bit boring so I determined to make the lunch club loud, exciting and the biggest and best club at the school. The venue was a little drama studio and I got four TVs hooked up to play videos (projectors were too expensive back then), had computer games and also did a bit of a 'God-slot'.

Do you feel that you have enough contact time with young people? What could you do to increase this relationship building time?

I was totally amazed that each lunchtime between 80 and 120 kids would show up, running to grab their lunch as soon as the bell went so they could be first in the queue to the club. One ridiculously easy thing I did to help with a sense of belonging was to give them a pass to the lunch clubs. It was just a piece of laminated cardboard with a number on it but there was virtually a riot from the kids trying to get hold of one! This small token told them that they had somewhere to belong. I very quickly had to rope in a few more local youth workers to help in the schools work as the size of the club would have been pretty unmanageable on my own. As the club grew and gained momentum I think there was a sense of shock from some of the teachers. They couldn't believe so many kids would want to go to a Christian club. It was an excellent start for my schools ministry.

This sense of belonging is an immensely powerful force. What could you do to increase the sense of belonging of your young people?

A few years later we'd met hundreds of young people through the school. People like Billy. We knew that there were restrictions on what we could tell them about Christ while they were in school, and desperately wanted to see these young people come to know

God as their father, and know that Jesus was passionate about their lives. The normal traditions and expressions of church were fairly inaccessible for these young people, whose attention spans would not cope with anything too long or too formal. The local churches got their heads together and we started something called Sound Service; an alternative expression of Church aimed at the young people. Multi media presentation, competitions, a young dynamic worship band, smoke machines and talks as relevant as possible all helped to make Sound Service a huge success. The service attracted around 300 young people each month, including many of the kids I was meeting in the school. We weren't allowed to advertise the service in the school but if people asked us what we did we'd tell them about Sound Service. Many of those guys came along. In the first year we saw 100 young people make a commitment. The Times newspaper also wrote an article on us titled "It's Christianity, but not as we know it."

Sound Service also brought about some amazing connections for me. Mike Coates from Ichthus Christian Fellowship led the music and worship for the meetings and I didn't realise it but Mike was on the same church leadership team as Simon Thomas, one of the teachers at Kingdale school where I was working. Simon and Mike asked me to consider starting some more schools work in Peckham, South London. I jumped at the chance, but initially found that the schools we approached were suspicious of anything connected with the Church. They assumed that any youth work provided by Christians would have an agenda of proselytisation that just wouldn't be appropriate in a school. However, sometimes it just takes a little time, slowly building relationships, for trust to grow. I explained time and again that we were part of a local church that wanted to serve the local community and were offering to serve the schools in any way we could. As the message began to sink in we found ourselves invited in to take lessons, give assemblies and help out in other ways.

One of the first schools in the area to take advantage of our offer was a school in the heart of Peckham. The school was incredibly ethnically diverse with over 65 language groups represented among the pupils. Many of these kids could speak very little English and found themselves marginalised within the school. Despite their normal intelligence, a great number of the pupils for whom English was a second language would do badly academically. As they frequently found themselves unable to understand their lessons they would often misbehave and be referred for disciplinary action. Sadly a high percentage of the young people would simply drop out of education altogether.

Recognising this unfortunately common scenario, we started helping students with English as their second language who were struggling to achieve their academic potential. Though it was time intensive, we simply sat with them every week and helped them to improve their reading skills. Dealing with multiculturalism was not as easy as I'd thought. It's one thing to be aware of the difficulties for these young people, and I could rattle off the statistics, but applying this knowledge to your work is a much bigger hurdle. I often fell victim to mistakes made as a teacher in a multicultural school.

I vividly remember one lesson I was teaching. I liked to think I was pretty good at controlling a class and keeping them quiet without resorting to raising my voice but on this particular day I was losing it. While I was trying to conduct a lesson on peer pressure, two boys behind desks at the back were hunched over, constantly whispering to one another. They'd been this way ever since I started and I'd had enough. "Will you two just be quiet!" I shouted at them. "Sorry sir," one replied quietly, "I'm just translating what you're saying for my friend so he can keep up. He's doesn't understand any English." That shut me up! In many classrooms this could be a good line to get away with chatting to a friend for an hour, but here in Peckham I knew it to be true.

Can you look back on mistakes that you have made which were painful at the time but which have taught you a lot?

I don't know if you've ever felt out of your depth. At this point in my life I was out of my depth in so many ways, learning about different cultures and trying to understand how to communicate across cultural divides. My dad had always taught me that effective communication was about stepping into someone else's world and seeing the world as they see it. You have to try to understand their experiences and where they are coming from, which is quite a challenge when you're from a white middle-class background working in a predominantly black Afro-Caribbean community. Often in a classroom I'd be faced with hostile faces whose expression said, 'What could you possibly know about my life?' It was intimidating and at times disheartening to think these kids had upbringings I couldn't even imagine, but I knew I wanted to find better ways to relate to them and certainly didn't want to be defeated because of the colour of my skin.

This desire to learn how to communicate in the most effective way, and understand the complex issues we face as youth workers in the multi-cultural world of South East London has taken me around the world. There is no better substitute for learning this than immersing yourself in that culture. In the early years of XLP I was lucky enough to meet Les Isaac, an inspiring, larger than life character involved in the Ichthus church. Les had moved to England from Antigua when he was young and experienced what it was like to grow up as a young black man in London. He did a lot to help me understand afro-Caribbean culture, and took me to Ghana and the Caribbean on mission, places that I have visited many times since. This knowledge has been crucial to us at XLP; the ability to communicate effectively is something we are always striving for. In a city as fast paced city like London we are on a constant learning curve. A grounding in the history and culture of other people and nations has given us a good foundation for engaging with young people, but you can't just leave it as that. We always need to listen to the young people and communities that we work with and learn from them, times change and our work needs to keep up.

What steps can you take to immerse yourself in the culture of the young people you minister to?

Our work in Peckham was so successful that I recruited another leader, Mike Godden. Even with someone to share the load, I was starting to realise that the level of need in Peckham alone was overwhelming. There were simply too many disadvantaged kids in the area for Mike and I to help. However, we saw the impact we had on some of the kids we worked with and this was enough evidence that their efforts were not in vain.

In one school which we worked in there was a young boy called Muhammad who was constantly bullied. The problem got so bad that Muhammad would climb a tree at the school gates, far above the other children's reach, and wait for us to arrive. When he saw my red Escort pulling into the car park he would climb down the tree and go into school feeling safe in the knowledge the 'the Christians' would protect him.

Together Mike and I began to develop a vision for our work that would see areas which had been written off and put down transformed. We wanted to bring hope to the most disadvantaged communities in South London. We started to broaden the list of lessons we taught in schools to tackle subjects like drug and alcohol abuse and crime – issues which had huge impacts in the area we were working.

In 1996, these initiatives were all brought together as a community project within the Ichthus Christian Fellowship. That's when XLP took on its name. Though I still had the responsibility of raising salaries and finding resources, having a name under which the work was carried out and a more structured support system allowed for our vision to be widened.

Realising that Peckham wasn't the only local community in need, we decided to spread XLP's net wider and began working in other areas of Southwark and the neighbouring boroughs of Lewisham and Greenwich. In order to staff this expansion a 'gap year' course was planned which invited school leavers to get involved in inner city mission for a year before they went to university. In its first year, the gap year added five extra members of staff to XLP and allowed our schools work to grow dramatically.

We were developing quite a reputation among the schools in our catchment area and, in contrast to the struggles that I'd had building trust and relationships with schools in the past, we found that schools would actually approach us to ask for help.

Around this time one of the initiatives that XLP had developed was really starting to gather momentum. We'd been looking for an activity that could run within schools that didn't favour any ethnic group. We wanted to find someway of bringing ethnically diverse youngsters together, uniting them in a common goal, but recognised the importance of such an event being a level playing field – something in which language skills and cultural background were not a hindering factor. We hit upon the idea of running a talent show, which turned out to be a roaring success.

After we'd seen how well the talent show went, it was decided we'd do a similar event in every school in the borough of Southwark. The best two acts from each school would go on to perform in a borough wide show in a local theatre. When the night of that final show arrived, 400 people were packed into the Civic Theatre on the Old Kent Road. It was incredible to see so many people coming out to celebrate the talent of local kids who were normally written off by society.

One of the kids who performed was called David and lived on the Aylesbury Estate – a typical South London high-rise with high unemployment, high crime rates, and low self-esteem. David played the bongos, a skill he had learned at school by tapping on the desks! He was an exceptionally gifted drummer – but none of the 20 members of his family who came to see him perform knew anything about his skill. After the show his father stood in front of the stage with tears in his eyes. He explained to one of the XLP staff that he had no idea that he could play so well. All he knew about his son was when one of the boy's teachers phoned up to say that he was in detention again. It was the first time that David's dad had known real pride in his son. It was an event that changed family relationships.

The talent shows were proving such a success that we decided to launch them in all of the boroughs in which they worked and, in 2000, held a South East London final show at Southbank University: a great next step in XLP's growth and a huge boost for the young people involved. Confidence and self-esteem were raised and, with a new drive and focus, the entrants found something that they could do in school that they enjoyed and were skilled in.

How could you find ways of showcasing the particular talents and gifts of the less celebrated members of your group?

Our work has grown and changed dramatically in our 13 year history. Lunch clubs, lessons, assemblies, reading support and the arts showcase are all still happening, but now we have the capacity to compliment that with community work, schools tours, arts training and a larger gap year course. As a personal journey it hasn't been without its struggles. Youth work can be very emotionally draining. You can be working hard and feeling like you are really getting somewhere with the young people, but when someone you have tried so hard to reach gets shot or ends up pregnant you feel like you're just a drop in the ocean, like you've achieved nothing. As well as this I've had to grapple with situations that have scared me, both in Trenchtown, Jamaica, and on my doorstep in Peckham. Fearing sometimes not just for myself but my family as well. In all this, though, I have known God's peace and pushed through the feelings that so easily could hold me back.

There are two developments at XLP that I never would have dreamed about running all those years ago when our work began.

The first is a slight departure from our South London focus. After my many trips to Ghana, first with Les and then every year with our gap year students, we've worked in schools, prisons and hospitals in the more remote heart of the great West African nation. We have grown a partnership with an amazing woman called Pastor Akousa, who runs the Ashanti-Akim Community Organisation and together we have raised enough money to build a school in the remote village of Danpong. Our vision has always been to work with those overlooked by others, and so placing the school hours from the capital, off the beaten track in an area often gripped by the hands of poverty, seemed to be what God was calling us to do. This school will change the lives of hundreds of young Ghanaians. We are sponsoring children, who wouldn't usually be able to afford the luxuries of an education, so that they can attend the school. It's taken years of seeing an area of dense jungle slowly transformed into a place of hope for young people but we are flying out to Ghana in September (2007) to see the school open; a school which has the potential to be one of the best in the country, in a small forgotten village in a vast nation.

The second development is Gunz Down – A project which tackles the worrying trend of knife and gun violence in London. We've teamed up with GreenJade, a Christian hip-hop group, after both realising that something needed to be done. I had just returned from Trenchtown, Jamaica, one of the world's murder capitals. I'd seen the terror of full scale gang violence and the way it has ravaged the community there. Rapper Wisdom, from GreenJade, had called because they had been in Birmingham performing only a few miles away from where two young girls had been murdered outside a New Year's Eve party. We agreed something positive needed to be done, and the Gunz Down tour was formed. The tour is a show followed by lessons that unpack the issues of gangs, gun and knife crime and making wise lifestyle choices. In a time when gun crime is becoming more common, and our local paper makes depressing reading, we are continuing to try and make what difference we can through the Gunz Down Tour.

Do you think that there are any potentially strategic new partners around that God might be wanting you to work with to extend the scope and impact of your ministry?

Rakeem is one young person who benefited from seeing the tour. He came up to us at the end of the show wearing a bulletproof vest. At first we thought he was messing about but we realised his fear was genuine when we heard that his cousin had been shot, his brother was lying in hospital and he'd been told a gang wanted to kill him. The Gunz Down show gave him an opportunity to be honest with us about how bad things had become in his life and how much serious trouble he'd found himself in. He was on the verge of converting to Islam – like many of the young people attracted by the strong sense of belonging and the passionate call to fight. Rakeem really affected me and I knew we had to do something to help. The fear haunted me that if we didn't it might not be long before he was dead. I called Les and asked his advice, once again feeling out of my depth. With his own experience of being involved with vicious gangs, Les said he'd be happy to mentor Rakeem, to get involved in his life and see if he could help him find a way out of his current mess. They now meet up regularly and Les even went to the police station when Rakeem was arrested – more than Rakeem's own dad was able to do as he was living in Jamaica.

Recently, as Rakeem was leaving school one afternoon, a member of a rival gang stabbed him in the throat. Charlotte (our Southwark team leader) received a phone call from a distraught Natalie (who works in his school) saying she was on her way to see him in the hospital. After they spoke to the doctors we found out the knife was millimetres away from hitting Rakeem's central nerves which would have left him seriously injured. We thanked God he was OK but obviously still have concerns over his safety. The amazing thing about this incident was that it prompted Natalie to hold a service at her church looking at gang issues. Eight of the kids from school came, deeply affected by seeing Rakeem attacked. There was space in the service for the young people to speak and say how things were from their point of view and one in particular told of how he felt holding a bleeding Rakeem in his arms, not knowing if he would live or die. The church elders prayed for all the young people and five of them gave their lives to Jesus. They still meet up with Natalie and Charlotte to chat about what it means to be a disciple of Jesus.

Though we have made lots of mistakes on the way, XLP is now running 60 lunch clubs every month, works in 35 different schools, and has seen thousands of young people go through the arts showcase. We've come to realise that it is sometimes the insignificant things we do that really make a big difference in the fight to bring hope to broken places.

For further reflection ...

Patrick Reagan writes, "I don't know if you've ever felt out of your depth. At this point in my life I was out of my depth in so many ways ..." He goes on to say, "In the early years of XLP I was lucky enough to meet Les Isaac."

Do you often feel out of your depth?

Do you believe that God can provide the people you need to encourage, support and help you develop in your ministry?

Are these people already in place, or do you need to prayerfully seek them out?

CHAPTER THIRTEEN

Re-sourcing Churches, Refreshing Young Lives

The Story of Hexham and Newcastle Youth Ministry Team

Fr. Dermot Donnelly

Looking back on the journey, it is only with hindsight that we realise how big the dream was some 12 or 13 years ago. Coming from the Catholic tradition, most dioceses throughout the country had a nominated 'youth officer' who was sometimes full time but, more often than not, part-time. At this time our diocese was no different from any other; however, the times were changing and a new way to reach out and support young people across our church was needed. If you were not a person of faith it would seem as if the events that happened were all a coincidence but the story that unfolds is about the realisation of a dream that was bigger than anyone could hope or imagine and it is obvious that it was truly inspired as the work of the Spirit.

Are you able to find the time and space to dream great dreams?

It was our dream to develop an effective, evangelistic, radical youth service within a Roman Catholic context and it gave birth to the Hexham and Newcastle Youth Ministry Team (YMT). Our strategy is three fold: firstly, bringing together an international group of young people to carry out missions; secondly, having a retreat centre (eventually to become a residential facility) where people could come and experience what it is to be community; thirdly, working with adults within the local parishes so that they can support young people on their journey.

We are known throughout our church as YMT and are now based on a 12 acre site outside the County Durham town of Consett. The site is a former market garden and stables converted into a country holiday let. We purchased the site in 2004 and, with a little imagination and little more cash, we carried out a few conversions so that the stone built cottages now house the international group of volunteers who live together in community, study, pray and minister to their peers. The centre also houses the offices for those employed fulltime by the diocese to work in youth ministry. The barn, which once stored the farm equipment, was converted into a state of the art auditorium which holds 120 people along with a new kitchen and dining room, a facility which we presently use for day retreats from schools across the North East.

The centre, known as the Youth Village, aims to be a place from where young evangelists take the message of the Gospel using modern mediums and present it to their peers working mainly in schools and parishes across the region. This group of evangelists, made up of the international volunteers and staff, also work throughout the country and within Ireland. We spend time during the year teaching a validated certificate in Theology and Youth Ministry in order to raise up leaders within our church.

I think it would be true to say that, as a Church, we Catholics have not been good at youth ministry outside of our schools. Within our denomination, our response in past years to working with young people was to build Catholic schools. It is also worth pointing out that, in its day, the building of faith schools was a most visionary and radical response to the needs of young people of that time. We must also remember that it was always meant to be in partnership with the home and the parish community. However at some level today, the presence of the schools can let the local church community 'off the hook' and they can blame the schools for the lack of church attendance. The schools do a fantastic job, and we have the pleasure of working in many of them, but this can only be one part of our ministry to young people. I feel it is essential that we see our ministry to young people as a partnership and each of the partners must take an active role.

Can you identify particular weaknesses in your church's or denomination's approach to work with young people? Identifying past weaknesses can be a great way towards creating future strengths.

It was for this reason that a number of years ago we decided to change how we would work as an organisation. Our three fold strategy offering mission experiences, follow-up retreats and also support for those within the local church was fine on paper. However, it was all out of sync. This was due largely to the fact that as an organisation we grew at different levels. We began solely as a youth mission team with a dream for the other elements to become a reality – which they did – but it happened over a period of 10 years. As a result of this gradual realisation of the strategy, it meant as an organisation we were reactionary. The phone would ring and it may be a school looking to book a mission or retreat or possibly a parish community somewhere looking to see what they could do about the lack of young people in their congregation. The phone calls would determine where we would work and the people to whom we would minister and we generally found we were working in the same places each year. A school or a group would pencil us in for the same week in the same term to work with their Year 8 group or 6th form group or to lead a retreat somewhere. This meant that a large number of schools, churches and communities in our diocese with whom we were commissioned to work would not get a chance to see us and we would not get a chance to minister to them.

Do you feel that you spend too much time 'reacting'? What could you do to become more purposeful?

We also found that the parish asking for support wasn't connected to the school seeking a mission which meant that there seemed to be no conversation between the partners about the need for youth provision. Neither were we acting as the necessary catalyst to facilitate, support and encourage holistic youth ministry. It was almost as if we were looking at the whole ministry in the short term: go to an area, preach the message and then go somewhere else and, the more we get out there, the better. Although on one level, I believe whole heartedly that the more opportunities we have to spread the Gospel the better, I also know that preparation and conversation with those with whom we are working would bear more fruit. It was important to stop looking at the ministry in the short term and begin to look at building for the future. The way we were functioning was almost like trying to plant seeds without first preparing the land and then leaving it up to chance that these seeds would grow; and then hope that someone somewhere would notice that the seed had begun to grow and would begin to nurture it.

This preparation time is vital in order to develop sense that it is the role of the whole church to care and encourage the faith of young people. Over the years we have worked with many 'partner' groups or as some call them, 'mission control.' I remember the first group we ever worked with, all the partners coming together, the school, the parishes local groups and ourselves as the facilitators. We met together an a church hall and the excitement was tangible. All off a sudden the question about what we do about young people was not one or two concerned people in an individual parish but now it was high on the agenda for the local community. People who had never met each other became good friends over a series of training weekends and this allowed the group to grow and develop new insights. The mission had a huge impact on the area and some four years later this group are still working in partnership with the school and have rallied support and finances to further develop the ministry to young people in their local community. They are now preparing for their next mission in two year's time.

This reactive way of working that we had found ourselves adopting in the early years also meant that we were running our team into the ground. It was hard to say 'No', even when it was getting to the point of being physically impossible to carry out the outreach. The staff members were stretched and the volunteers also were working at an incredible rate. I think this reluctance or even fear to say 'No' was for a number of reasons something to do with our history.

When the team first began, it would be true to say that it came out of the Catholic Charismatic Renewal Movement. The Charismatic Renewal movement hit the Catholic Church in England around the 70s and, as a result, especially in the eighties and nineties, there were a number of communities and ministries developing. These new communities led by the Spirit were mostly young people and their charism was generally evangelisation. It was one such community carrying out a mission in a school in our diocese that spurred the bishop at the time to set up a mission team in 1995. It was unusual within the mainstream Catholic Church to have such an organisation working fully as part of the diocesan structures. It was truly the Charismatic and the Institution coming together and allowing that healthy tension to determine the vision and strategy for the future.

And so the dream was born, but, as you could imagine, it was received within the Church with much suspicion: What would it be? What would it do? How was it going to talk to young people about Jesus? How much would it cost? And the list went on. This meant that from day one we needed to somehow become a credible organisation that would be respected by the institution without losing anything of its charism. It was radical and it needed to remain such; indeed, the word radical comes from the word 'root', and somehow this new organisation was getting back to the roots and taking as its mandate the great commission given to the Church: "Make disciples."

Do you spend enough time communicating and demonstrating the credibility of your work to church leaders and building the reputation of your ministry?

The 'suspicion' of how our organisation would work within the church was not only within our local region but also by youth ministry providers in dioceses around the country.

We knew, however, that the respect, the credibility and the trust would come from the encounters we would have with those who engaged with us and the stories they would tell to others about the outreaches they had experienced. So we began feeling we were meant to be, but also feeling we had something to prove and to convince people about. Our future existence would depend on getting this right and we had to very quickly build up not just a good reputation but a reputation beyond reproach. We would only be as good as our last outreach or our last mission.

These were what we called our nomadic years; as well as carrying out the work we also moved house six times in ten years. As we continued to grow, a bigger house was needed in order to allow the ministry to exist and empty church properties would become available and we would move on to our new home. These years were important times as it meant we travelled the region and allowed people to meet us at all different kinds of levels. It was not until 2004 that the diocese bought our present facility, the Youth Village, a sign that those early years of pioneering and gaining credibility had paid off.

From all over young people attend activities at the Youth Village and in other places that we provide a more focused experience. Each year we run a 'Summer Festival' which could be seen as one big retreat. It is during school time and about 16-18 schools take part. The young people are mainly aged 15-17 years old and from a variety of different backgrounds and experiences. A lot of these young people would not have had much of an experience of what we may refer to as a worship setting. The main problem of the event is that it is limited and therefore it can only cater for under 300 participants which mean the places go like hot cakes. Not only do those who went in previous years wish to return, new people get to hear about it. It is normally up to me to set the scene and introduce the theme on the first night in the large marquee. After group builders, small groups, the 'guidelines' and the pep talk, the Festival kick starts with some lively worship and the opening talk. It is always a concern of how it may go because most of these young people would have not had an experience of this particular prayer style. However, to return the following night after the prayer and ministry experience you would think that they had been worshipping this way all their lives. One participant who had never been to anything like it before wrote down her thoughts about her experience.

> *"Over the couple of days we were there we took part in different activities! including Prayer and Mass – everything we did, the core of it was about God. We were told we didn't have to pray, or do anything that we didn't want to, as long as we didn't disrespect other people's choices but it wasn't a problem because we wanted to, whether we were praying normally or praying through song." (Summer festival participant, 2007)*

What is truly inspiring to me as someone who ministers to young people is how well young people respond to an authentic presentation of the Gospel and the person of Jesus.

> *"After two days camping, it was time to say our goodbyes. It rained everyday, there were spiders everywhere; it was cold, and we took part in a lot of prayer and you know what? It wasn't actually that bad, in fact it was fantastic!" (Summer festival participant, 2007)*

The challenge for us is always how we consolidate the experience that these young people have had. I am aware that this experience is a profound and real experience of the presence and the love of God. I know this not only because I can see it on the faces of the young when the 'penny drops' but also because they later articulate it as best as they can, using words that are unable to truly express how they felt, but somehow the need is there to have a stab at it. Numerous emails, evaluations and cards are received with many different words but always saying something of the same thing; "I experienced God!"

> *"The words God and Prayer are often said to disperse a crowd of teenagers faster than a police siren – but this was a wonderful occasion; a wonderful exception; and a memorable experience." (Summer festival participant, 2007)*

The tension is between getting the message out there and allowing young people to have such experiences and also creating an environment within their local community where there faith can be nurtured. The easiest is allowing them the experience and this was another reason why as an organisation we often responded generously with any and every invitation to work with young people.

However in time this reactive way of working with its consequent effort, energy and time, which still only catered for the 'short term', meant that we approached those in the diocese who had been appointed as our management team by the bishop, and suggested we wanted a major overhaul. A generous donation in the millennium year from a trust meant that we could begin to employ people and begin to move beyond just operating as a mission team. We had gone from simply providing missions to offering professional consultancy for clergy and members of the church congregations along with training and formation of adults and youth evangelists. Two strands of our strategy had been realised; all we needed now was to begin to have confidence and know that we had earned the credibility within our own diocese and were an essential and respected ministry within the institution. We were also aware that nationally, and subsequently internationally, within the Catholic world we were offering support to other bishops and services throughout the church by sharing our story.

The developments had demanded that we could not continue on the way we were going; everything had to be focused on a long term process which would encourage all the partners whose responsibility it is to pass on the faith to our young people to begin talking with each other.

In the Baptism service we find the words 'The Christian community welcomes you with great joy.' It was important for us to be conversing with the whole community and not working in a vacuum. There is a Ghanaian proverb 'It takes a whole village to raise a child' and I believe in Ghana there are only two types of people within a village; a parent or a child. It doesn't matter if you have children or not, each adult is a parent and has the responsibility to support the growth of every child's development. And so we could equally say that it takes a whole Church to raise a child and if we, as a Christian community, do truly 'welcome with great joy' then we must engage as a unified body providing opportunities and support for our young people.

Is youth ministry a whole church endeavour where you are or is the youth work working in a vacuum? What might you be able to do to improve the situation?

We knew this new overhaul would need some big steps and so in 2001-2002 we took a year of consolidation which allowed us to plan for the future. Our three fold strategy was going to be exercised by the development of a process which would engage all the partners in the mission and follow-up experience. For 12 months before the mission experience we gather all the 'partners' together; local schools, parish clergy, families and members of the worshipping community. Thus begins a discussion of how we provide more relevant opportunities for our young people. Step two of the process is the mission experience with a radical presentation of the gospel message for all young people and their families. The next step is looking at the follow-up and how we build on the mission experience. With this ongoing process the follow-up soon becomes the preparation for the next mission experience.

To date we run a full time mission team made up of international volunteers and provide them with training and formation whilst they minister to their peers. We have developed strong international networks mainly across the States and Australia as we discern the direction in which we need to develop for the future. At the heart of it all, there is the development of the youth village, providing centre-based teaching and formation. The support of adults, clergy and parents at local level is a key part of our ministry helping support the Church in general as we journey on as a pilgrim people.

Some people ask me how effective the work that we do is in any real sense and I am unable to answer that because I am convinced that we are called to sow the seed and that maybe the harvest is not ours to reap. However, what I do know is that over the last years that YMT has been functioning, people's lives have been changed and they have gone on to change others' lives – some of them we know of, some we will find out about at a later date and some we will never know. Working in this ministry, we can never measure where the Spirit will move and neither can we control it and so we simply do our bit. We enter into partnership with the Lord and hand it all over at the end of each day.

For further reflection ...

Father Dermott Donnelly finishes his story by saying: "Working in this ministry, we can never measure where the Spirit will move and neither can we control it and so we simply do our bit. We enter into partnership with the Lord and hand it all over at the end of the day."

Are you able to remember that the mission and the responsibility for the mission are God's and are you able to hand the work to him at the end of the day and sleep soundly and peacefully?

If not, what steps can you take to share the load with others and, ultimately, to rest in God's peace?

CHAPTER FOURTEEN

A lesson learned – the challenges of developing a schools project

The story of Luton Churches Education Trust

Chris Curtis

Visitors always head for a town's centre when they arrive somewhere new. It's an instinct, based on the belief that here they will find the heart of the place, what makes it tick. It's a fallacy of course – all they'll find are the same shops and stores that exist in their own town. To really understand the heart of a town, you have to walk some of the streets that lead away from the centre, passing through different housing stock like the rings on a tree, from the thirties semis through to the sixties council estates and beyond to the newer, smaller private houses built in the last few decades. As you do this you'll find the people and history of the place, the real heart.

One place this couldn't be more true is Luton, an industrialised town slightly out of kilter with the surrounding green and genteel countryside of Bedfordshire. The shopping centre had its glory days nearly forty years ago and can't help but look its age. But it would be unfair to judge it on those terms. In reality it's a thriving multicultural community of nearly two hundred thousand people, with perhaps more than its fair share of churches. (There are just over one hundred in all.) Although many occupy substantial buildings, fewer have congregations that fill them. Like anywhere else in Britain today, it's a challenge not to be consumed by the

need to sustain themselves, and to find the vision and means to engage with the local community.
Even so, many do, and in significant ways. Luton churches put on senior citizens' lunches, run social work projects, and provide support for those migrating here from Eastern Europe. Not surprisingly, young people are often cited as being a crucial target group in this challenge, though they often seem to be the hardest to reach. Perhaps they are less tolerant of our motives; they're certainly more likely to speak up if they're bored or unimpressed. Whatever the reason, fewer than five hundred of the fifteen thousand teenagers in Luton have any connection with a church, regardless of whether that definition of 'connection' includes attendance of a service, a youth group or even hanging out in an open youth club. It's a challenge only the bravest churches would want to take on and try to bring about change.

I moved here over a decade ago, and like everyone else, headed for the town centre to see what Luton might have to offer. No shock then, to find the answer was little different from anywhere I'd been before. Despite that, I took a job launching an inter-church youth project and becoming its first full-time worker. That was in 1993. By good fortune and the grace of God, I had no idea either of the challenge coming my way, or that so many years later I would still be part of this community. If we knew what would happen in the future, I'm not sure anyone would ever take risks that might lead to failure. And if we never failed, we'd never learn anything worth knowing. It turns out that ignorance has its advantages.

Not far from the rather bland shopping centre, along a road leading out past the older and altogether grander town hall, there's an old hat factory, a three-floored brick building with a history that had long since passed from making hats to become a dance studio and then, back in the 1980s, an office. When I first noticed it, walking past one Spring day, it had been derelict for five years and the 'for lease' sign was looking tattered and rather grubby. Set back from the road and behind some shops, it was easy to miss. The only reason I saw it was because I was looking for it. Not 'it' specifically, but for a place to develop the youth project and give us the space we needed. I'd been walking up and down those streets for an hour looking at old shops and empty offices. As it turned out, this old building was perfectly suited and moving in would become a key moment in our story. But that's getting ahead of ourselves – this was 1999, six years after the project started. Some explanation of how we got to that point is needed.

Beginnings

The project I joined had a vision to reach out to young people, but was a little less clear on the 'how'. Having moved to Luton only a few weeks after my first visit, I found myself wondering what that 'how' should look like. Churches were understandably keen to see fresh young people coming into their congregations, but making contact with them seemed a huge challenge.

As it was to turn out, connecting with young people was to be the easy part of the mission. They were more open-hearted, welcoming and friendly than most churches would have dared to imagine. But sharing faith in a way that was relevant to their lives, let alone drawing them into faith and discipleship, was to be a much bigger issue.

I remember walking across a housing estate in the north of the town with a young lad, Jonny, who was fourteen or fifteen. He'd been a persistent truant from school and even more trouble when he did turn up. We'd first met through the project's work in his school, providing counselling and mentoring for wayward students. His willingness to chat with me had taken me by surprise when we first sat down on one of the rare days when he'd turned up at school, and I happened to catch him. If he was put off by my connection with Christian faith and the church he didn't let it show. Instead he talked openly and honestly about what was going on in his life. Broken family relationships and a brother in trouble with the police had started the truancy. Now he'd lost so much time and got so far behind, a fear of looking stupid in front of the other students stopped him from going back to classes.

Now, a few months later, walking across that estate with him, I was struck by how easy it had been to make contact with a young person like Jonny who seemed so unreachable to many churches. His openness to honest genuine friendship, even from adults like myself, was a sign of a deeper and more positive character than is sometimes seen by the teacher or police officer who has to deal with their behaviour. But even so, sharing faith with Jonny, and seeing any new faith ignite, seemed a much greater challenge.

If our experience over the past few years has been about anything, it's been the story of how we took on that challenge. It would be great to be able to report success on a grand scale. In truth, I would be lying if I did. Where there has been change in a young person, it's been both precious and of infinite value but, in terms of numbers, it's been a trickle more than a flow. In Biblical terms, our work has more in common with Noah – one hundred and twenty years and only a handful find faith – than Jonah – three days and whole city turns to God.

Challenges

Amber, a fourteen year old in Luton, is who I visualise when I think of this challenge. Once met, never forgotten: there are teachers, youth workers and police who will remember this young woman for years to come. Her blond hair and fresh face could darken in an instance if anyone dared cross her and, on closer scrutiny, there was a weathered life-weary look about her that told a story of its own. Like Jonny, she had an absent father and a mother who struggled to keep control and curfew. In the company of older teenagers on the sprawling north Luton estate where she lived, Amber was an early-adopter of cigarettes and alcohol, and a permanent fixture in the Head Teacher's office at the local secondary school. She was a handful in any context, but also warm, funny and endearing to those who managed to get to know her.

I first came face to face with her myself on a summer residential week, where I was leading and Amber was, well, complaining. By the second day she, along with a cohort of co-conspirators, had begun a revolt over the food being offered and we ended up in a stand-off one evening with threats to go home on her part, and be sent home on mine. In the end we sat together and talked, with Amber insistent that a McDonalds or, at the very least, chips and gravy, needed to be on the menu, and that Shepherds Pie should be taken off with immediate effect.

I have to admit to being silently impressed by Amber's forthrightness. I was much quieter myself as a teenager, and sometimes wished I had been louder, or at least more assertive. But if Amber wasn't happy, was bored or simply didn't like what was going on, she would tell you about it. With the issue of food resolved, the rest of the week went by with only the occasional confrontation. It had, I suspect, been a bit of a test, to figure out what we were like and how resolutely we would hold to our boundaries. Away from her gang, like many other troubled teenagers, Amber was far more reasonable and engaging than you might first have imagined, and once there was mutual respect, there was co-operation of sorts.

For me, Amber encompasses the basic challenge I face as a youth worker. If Christianity, let alone church, is to make its mark among teenagers today, it has to make sense to young people like Amber. Her bright, chaotic world is where Christianity has to show itself to be relevant and comprehendible. And her world, with her friends and family, is where any new-found faith has to find a place to grow and blossom.

Of course I have no doubt that Jesus is wholly relevant and that the Christian faith, in its purest form, is up to the challenge. Whether I can communicate the faith well enough is another matter – as is the question of whether we, the church, can even begin to understand the scale of the challenge, let alone succeed in helping young people like Amber grow in faith.

I still have, as a reoccurring nightmare, the memory of a young skinhead in the early 80s turning up to our church for the first time as a new Christian in an ill-fitting suit. The mistake of the church had not been that they'd encouraged him to do so – it had been his idea based on his impression of what the church would expect - but that they hadn't told him to ditch the suit and come in whatever he felt comfortable in the following week. Like many young people who come to faith, he lasted a few months and then drifted away. The look of discomfort on his face during that first service has stayed with me and serves to remind me how important it is to think hard about how we enable young people to engage with the church community.

Surprises

Much of our work over the years has been in local schools, where Christian mission needs an educational as well as a theological rationale. Evangelism seems inappropriate in the classroom, where debate and questions are more suited. That is not to say our ministry was without spiritual fruit. Alongside the lessons and assemblies, we ran youth events, weekends away and summer camps, drawing together young people from local churches and some of those we had got to know in school. The team grew too, with new staff and volunteers, and three or four years in there were six of us working together.

One element common to all our events and camps was a challenge for young people to reach a point of decision about the Christian faith. Whilst some of it seems manipulative looking back, it seemed much more straightforward at the time. Our connections with churches made passing on young people easier and we could relax in the knowledge that youth leaders would be inviting any new Christians to church the following Sunday. If numbers were important, we certainly had success in these early days with young people finding faith and joining churches.

I will always remember the 23rd of September 1994 as being one evening when we saw success of this kind in an astonishing way. It was the first major youth event we had held, in the one of the largest town-centre churches. We had worked through the afternoon setting up a stage, adding lighting and putting the PA system on steroids. In the background I had watched others practising sketches whilst a group of young musicians got ready to play.

Being in charge can feel uncomfortable at the best of times, but on a night like this it felt like a heavy burden. As evening approached, I began getting more and more nervous about who, if anyone, would come. The wooden chairs, which some years back had replaced the dark and heavy pews, were in straight rows across the nave of this grand old parish church. I remember pushing row after row further apart wondering if the greater space between them would create an impression of more people present. Then, just as we were about to walk around the back of the church towards the offices and vestry to pray, the minister tapped me on the shoulder and, with a wry smile, beckoned me outside into the churchyard. I walked out wondering what disaster I might face but instead, along the path, out onto the street and into the distance, was a line of young people who, it turned out, numbered just over a thousand. It took my breath away. Instead of pulling those seats apart, we pushed them uncomfortably close, added new rows, borrowed pew cushions to become seats and spent nearly an hour just getting people inside. That evening was a glorious moment, a sense that we were making a difference. And, to top it all, a huge number surged forward at the end, responding to the speaker's challenge. It was a triumph.

Other events followed, together with summer camps, weekends away and more. It was a fantastic few years and there is no doubt that God met with many of those young people in life changing ways. I see now that we relied too heavily on presenting from the front, gave too little space for questions, and put too much emphasis on public commitments. But God is gracious and overrules our mistakes. Nothing is wasted, even if time and wisdom show it to be less than it seemed in the moment.

However, looking back now, there's another perspective to what happened that doesn't, I believe, diminish the good of what we did, but does remind me of the bigger challenge we needed to face. The young people who came to those events were, by and large, the young people who were already connected with a church together with their friends. They were already open to what the Christian faith might be saying and they represented, on the whole, a more affluent and well-behaved cohort. They were not Amber or her friends nor, if we're honest, did they represent the majority of young people in the town.

What I mean by that is the sense that we, probably quite rightly, started work with the easiest and most open group of young people. They laughed heartily at our jokes and they listened mostly in silence to speakers share the message of the Christian faith. It was easy to give them follow-up material in the form of a booklet and there was no literacy barrier in encouraging them to start reading the Bible regularly. To share faith with them was important, but they were not the biggest challenge. Somewhere outside of the church that evening were young people who came from families with less money and little or no contact with a church and who were less comfortable listening for long periods to adult speakers.

It took us a while to see beyond the excitement of our event programme and realise that the results we were seeing were not the whole story. I wish I could say we were more perceptive and had greater honesty but, in truth, a few years passed before the reality began to gnaw at our conscience enough for us to notice.

When we did finally begin to think this challenge through, it proved harder than we imagined. It came to a head on a summer residential, a week away with just over a hundred of the young people who had either met us at school or been to an event. On this camp we had a much wider cross-section of young people than in the past. Although this was well before Amber appeared in our work, there were plenty of other teenagers with a similar experience and outlook. Coping with their behaviour quickly became a huge issue as it was clear that our programme – from food to evening meetings – didn't meet their approval and that they were going to make sure we realised this was the case. I remember struggling to deal with conflict after conflict, sending some young people home in disgrace and battling through the week with others. We came home dispirited and dejected, having seen few young people respond to our message, and with the clear message from the school where we had been staying, who were left with a few too many repairs, that we would no longer be welcome back in future years.

And yet, despite the difficult circumstances, it actually proved to be a key turning point in our work. We were no longer able to ignore the fact that our strategies and programmes didn't work for the majority of young people. We had to face what that meant for our mission and figure out what we should be doing instead. Together we felt a clear message from God that our priority had to be towards those with less, those at the 'bottom of the pile'. In America there's a youth programme that promotes the idea, as a method for evangelism, that you should find the most popular, sporty, good-looking young person in a school and try to convert them. The concept is that, if they find faith, they will bring many of their peers with them. It's called the 'key kid' strategy. In Luton we began to wonder if God was asking to do the opposite: find the most needy and oppressed and care for them. I guess you might still call it the 'key kid' strategy, but from a different theological perspective.

Changes

In 1999, the project began a new chapter in its story. Now with eleven staff, we set about changing the way we worked to give greater priority to young people in need. Central to our plans was finding a bigger and more suitable space than the cramped offices we occupied at the back of a church building. And so I found myself searching for somewhere to make that possible, and finding it that day, as I looked up at the old hat factory. Here, across three floors, we had enough space to dream of something different, a place where young people could hang out and find community, including Christian community. An army of volunteers and some generous local companies helped us over the next year take on this challenge and bring that dream into reality, creating a venue complete with cafe, art studio and enough space for our growing team to work from.

Physical changes were just the beginning. Theological and missiological change was needed too. We had to think about how we shared our faith with young people, and what would make sense to their life and experiences. We also had to figure out where our role ended and where local church's started. Passing young people on to churches from camps and events was hit-and-miss at the best of times. For every young person I could name who was part of a church youth group as a result of our ministry, there were far more who had started coming along to groups but withered away. Even the harsh statistics Jesus lays out in the parable of the sower didn't account for the drop-out rate, and I suspect we're not the only group of youth workers to face that issue either.

The youth centre gave us the ideal context in which to meet young people from the town who'd never been near a church. Throughout our experiences in Luton, meeting and befriending young people has never been the challenge. When our youth club opened its doors for the first time in September 2000, we found ourselves inundated with young people who were bored of walking up and down the shopping centre opposite and liked the idea of a place to hang out, even if it was something to do with Christians. We found ourselves running the club not only after school, but at weekends too. It was exhausting and challenging, but lots of fun too. For every confrontation quietened there were many great moments spent chatting with young people, playing pool or ruling as supreme champion of simple games like 'Connect 4'. We began to notice that our clientele included fewer and fewer church young people. They came at first out of curiosity and through our connections with local youth groups. But they were busy with their own youth schedules and our club soon became the province of a tougher, slightly more challenging kind of young person. There's also no doubt that for some church parents, seeing their child associate with some of these teenagers was a huge threat. Time after time we saw young Christian teens pulled away from our work because they might find themselves hanging out with an undesirable crowd. As a parent I can relate to that instinct to protect, but at the same time, it meant that few of the young people we worked with have the chance to see faith lived out in a peer. Instead, it was left to us as adult youth workers to provide the role model. It works, but it's far from ideal.

Struggles

Standing in the corner of the cafe one evening, I watched our team as they sat alongside a group of young people. There was Simon, sitting talking with a young lad who I knew had just seen his father walk out the door. A group of girls played cards with Janice: if only they were this engaging and co-operative at school. And there, playing pool, was another of our team, Andrew. He was talking to a young lad whose hood was still drawn up over his head and who looked slightly unkempt and, I thought, forlorn. These were young people from the local estates who were happy to spend their time with us instead of roaming the street. It was both a privilege and a huge challenge to think that we were called to live out our lives and faith in their company. There's no doubt that incarnational youth work, living out the presence of Jesus, is at the heart of Biblical youth ministry.

Even so, this was still far from where we needed to be. Over the past few years our work had shifted to focus much more on young people far outside the church. Some were broken by their life experience, many were known to be trouble at school. Still others didn't bother to go at all. Our team had begun to get to know a group of these young people, and the cafe and new building we had moved into was a great help in making that happen. But befriending a young person wasn't the end of the story. We wanted to share our faith openly with them, talking about the person who had changed us and who we now followed in our lives.

That's where the next challenge kicked in. Looking around that evening, I realised that those young people had literally no knowledge of the Christian faith, not even a distant echo through sitting in a Sunday school. These were teenagers without even the language to express or understand spiritual experience. Ask any of them if they were spiritual and they'd just as likely think you were talking about whether they'd seen a ghost. Something clicked in me at that moment. Incarnating the life of Christ was vital – of course it was, and we were never going to stop doing that – but if we were to help these young people interpret what they saw in us, even if it was only to decide we were all completely deluded, we needed to help them find the words to explain it.

The young people we were working with didn't use words like grace or salvation, or even prayer, in their ordinary language. They didn't talk about worship or 'being at peace'. Even the concept of hope would have been alien to many of them. And even if they knew what those words meant, and not all would have done, they would find it hard to understand what these concepts had to do with them. At the same time, there's no doubt that most of them would have had spiritual experiences. OK, not at the same level as Paul heading to Damascus, but perhaps a sense of a connection with something deeper at a family funeral, or a feeling of being part of some greater plan as they sat one evening on holiday and watched the sun go down over the sea. Those moments may have been 'spiritual' but none of the young people we were working with would have known them in those terms.

As we talked this through as a team, we wrestled with what it meant to help a young person find a spiritual voice. Not simply learning theological words, but finding the ability to express themselves in spiritual terms. One of the moments that can most clearly into focus was a few years later, as the dreadful tsunami hit much of Asia on 26 December 2004. When the schools opened a week or so later, the world was still in shock at the devastation and loss of life and, not surprisingly, many schools organised collections to raise money to help.

Breakthrough

It's often at moments of tragedy or great loss, whether on this global scale or personally, that spiritual questions and yearnings are thrust to the fore. In those first few day of the term, we talked together as a team and began to realise that young people across the town needed some way to express what they were feeling – not just emotionally or financially, but spiritually as well. But what could we do? Someone had an idea. We should hold a service for teenagers, a space where they could do just that. It seemed just right, and so we set about putting it together. A few days later, crowded into the cafe after school, I looked around at a group of young people – not exactly thousands but enough to fill the place – as we began a forty five minute service on the theme of the tsunami. I gulped and got ready to see what would happen. These were young people who didn't go to church, but the scale of the tragedy had pulled them to this place to respond to God about what was happening. It was hard to know what to expect or what they would make of it.

Perhaps by accident more than design, we'd included a couple of approaches in the service that turned out to work perfectly (though neither of them were particularly new or unique). One was the use of symbolic ritual, in this case lighting candles and placing them on a large map of the world we'd created with masking tape on the black lino of the cafe floor. It seems ridiculously simple, but somehow in the action of placing a candle and perhaps whispering a prayer to a God who you weren't even sure existed, something profound could happen for a young person: a spiritual experience.

The second was to use liturgy, written prayers often with repeated responses. On the team, our Christian traditions tended to only use 'spontaneous' prayer with a slight suspicion of anything that was prepared as being somehow less spiritual. In the event, we had put together some simple prayers ourselves, read from the front but with repeated responses so that everyone could take part. It worked. If we had simply let the room fall quiet and asked people to pray out loud if that wanted to, I bet not a single young person would have uttered a syllable. I can remember myself as a young Christian feeling a bag of nerves at the thought of praying out loud – and that was only in a small house group! Instead, using this approach everyone took part in some way. It seemed more holistic and I certainly felt God's presence standing in the corner of the cafe that winter evening.

Looking back now, I realise lots of things were happening that day. For one, the barrier between youth worker and young person was broken down. Instead of the 'adults' putting something on for the young people, we were worshipping and praying together, as equals of sorts. And those young people could see us for the first time in the cafe not playing pool or Connect 4, but engaging with Jesus. These teenagers were part of something spiritual. The words we chose to use were simple enough, but there's no doubt that anyone coming along that evening would have had a taste of what it might look like to express yourself spiritually as a Christian.

That service was a breakthrough for us in the way we thought about sharing our faith. In those forty five minutes, no one made a plea for commitment or asked anyone to put their hand up to become a Christian and no one explained the gospel with funny stories and teen-friendly jokes. And yet I couldn't remember a time when I thought we'd shared the heart of the Christian faith so clearly as when we prayed together that evening, confessing that we understood little of why such a tragedy had happened and yet we had faith in God despite it. That night, something transformed the way we were doing ministry, and it changed everything.

The following wet summer, we'd found a new school willing to risk having us as guests for a week's residential and took just over forty young people away for the holiday of their lives. It was also to be the week I met Amber, and experienced the full impact of her forceful personality. Building on the ideas we'd stumbled on in January, we designed a programme that used ritual and liturgy, gave space to questions and interaction and, to top it all, used a three-hundred-year-old story – Bunyan's *Pilgrim's Progress* - as its theme. The 'me' of a few years back would have looked on in horror and wondered if we'd get past the first day.

We did. We saw young people finding a spiritual voice, being able to describe themselves in spiritual language, and using simple rituals to connect with God. We even saw a group decide to become Christians. Not the big numbers we might have seen through our old style, with more pushy preaches. But these young people seemed to have connected on a deeper level with themselves as well as with God. It was a promising start.

Deeper

Somewhere under the floor of our cafe back in Luton, was a basement used for storage and, to be frank, dumping old and unwanted bits and pieces. Boxes of lost property from old weekends away nestled in the darkness with paints pots and off-cuts of wood. It was a place you tended to avoid, and the damp peeling walls of the narrow stairs that led down to it from the kitchen were in stark contrast with the refurbished cafe. For some reason I found myself standing in this basement one Monday afternoon, looking for something and wondering who, other than myself, could be persuaded to tidy up the mess. And then, standing there looking around, an idea dropped into my mind that seemed at first crazy, expensive and ridiculous.

Coming back from our summer camp, we knew the direction our ministry was taking us. We needed to find more ways for young people to engage with God themselves instead of listening to us talk about it. Out with the epilogues and fancy youth events; in with opportunities for teenagers to meet with God themselves. The tsunami service had shown that they would turn up to spiritual events – in fact, they seemed keener on those than the wacky stunt-driven youth events we had run a decade before. And so, looking round that basement, an idea was born. We would create a chapel, a spiritual space, where young people from the cafe could come and pray or be quiet ... or do whatever they needed to do to connect with God. We could hold services, not just to cope with tragedies, but regularly, and we would give the young people coming to the cafe a way to explore Christian spiritual life.

It took just over a year for that dream to become a reality, and as I write this, we are admittedly only at the beginning of this next stage in our journey. The chapel is finished: rubbish and old props long since cleared out, walls painted, new lights and carpet installed. The old dingy stairs are now a great deal more enticing and as you head down them and turn into the basement room, you see a very different sight. Centre stage is a large metal cross, nearly five foot high, imposing a sense of the spiritual purpose of this space. The cross isn't solid, it's fifty words soldered together and shaped. The words have come from fifty local young people who were asked to describe their life. Some are positive, even joyful; others are more negative and despairing. I like to imagine that the metaphor is clear, Christ dwells among the pain, the struggles and the hopes of these young people.

We've also appointed a chaplain, someone who will oversee this place and help the young people who come here. And we're nearly six months into having weekly services where young people, together with the team, sit side by side, sharing life and finding faith. I'm not going to pretend the results are immediate or even impressive. Numbers fluctuate and I wish Luton was small enough that people didn't need to take a bus to get here. It makes it harder especially when the weather is bad. But despite this, there's a sense that this is where God has taken us in our mission to share faith with some of the toughest young people in Luton. Even Amber has been a few times.

The chapel complements the work we continue to do in local schools, where most of our time is still spent. It feels like we've found the missing component in what we've been trying to do. Of course there are plenty of issues. We're not trying to run a 'church' in the normal sense of the word and it's not meant to replace the churches in the town. But young people may find their home here for a while before making it to one of those churches. It's not a neat system, and I'm sure there'll be issues about how young people can connect to a church long term. But you have to start somewhere, and it's working. The walls of the chapel are now covered with prayer requests and there's a feeling we've only just seen the beginning of what is going to happen.

Of course, the irony is laughable. Set up by local churches who ran services full of ritual and liturgy but empty of young people, we have, after fourteen years of trying other things, ended up running services full of liturgy and ritual in a chapel. Perhaps the church wasn't as far away from young people as we thought.

POSTSCRIPT

Thinking Without Limits for Church Unlimited

Jonathan Brant

This is a trustworthy saying that deserves full acceptance (and for this we labour and strive), that we have put our hope in the living God, who is the saviour of all humanity, and especially of those who believe.
(1 Timothy 4 vs 9-10)

Introduction (Or, Why We Should Treasure the Questions)

And so, we come to the close of our journey together. In this final chapter I would like to reflect upon the remarkable stories that we have read and to consider the impact that these stories might have on the way we think about our faith and the way we live-out our calling to be the body of Christ to young people, with young people and alongside young people. In other words, I would like to engage in some thinking without limits in the hope that it might help us to develop as a church without limits.

If you've worked with young people for any length of time, then chances are you've been faced with the possibility, or even the reality, of physical violence. Contributors to this book have spoken of weapons fashioned from snooker balls twirled in threadbare socks, of stabbings, beatings-up and even deaths. I remember being in church one Sunday evening when one of the young people rushed up to me and told me that he had "accidentally" picked a fight with a local kid and that that kid was about to return with his mates to cause some serious trouble. I laughed ... until I walked outside and saw at least twenty teenagers from the local estate heading up the road towards me armed with bricks and bats. But I lived to tell the tale and the truth is that youth ministry, when you do it for real – when you open yourself up, when you allow yourself to feel something of what young people feel, when you dare to look at the world, the church, and at God with their eyes – confronts us with greater challenges than the occasional threat of violence. Real youth ministry makes us re-think what we thought we knew about God, about mission and about our place and purpose in the world.

A number of the contributors to this book speak movingly of this kind of challenge. Gary Bishop explains that, "During the seven years which have passed since I moved to Openshaw I have learned many things, not just in the practice of youth work but things about myself, about the world and about God. I've gained a very different understanding of what mission is." (p. 21) Helen Gatenby, who has spent 18 years serving on one estate, admits that, perhaps, over that time she has changed more than anything around her. You might remember how she wrote of her struggle:

> *Early on, I clearly remember a point where I felt I faced a stark choice theologically, and I'm probably not alone in this. Two or three years into the work, I had seen none of the revival I'd been led to expect would happen when we 'trust God, give our lives and set out to work for him'. Signs and wonders were evident in churches in other more affluent areas of the country, but it wasn't happening here. I asked myself, "Have I got it right theologically, and God*

> *just isn't here with the poor and marginalised, as I don't see any evidence of him as I was told I would", or "Is God here with the poor and marginalised, and I can't yet see it and have got it wrong theologically." Either large parts of my faith had to make room for change or I had to give up on God being interested in the poor and leave. But I could not abandon my belief that God loves the poor and so I let go of parts of my theological framework, sought God and stayed.*

Helen's words resonate powerfully with me because I've struggled with similar questions, particularly after moving to South America and working with some severely troubled and marginalised young people. But, to be honest, the same questions had been bubbling just beneath the surface even while I worked in the far more comfortable environs of church-based, suburban youth ministry in the US and the UK. I firmly believe that such struggles and questions are to be treasured, not to be brushed under the carpet or shied away from. I am convinced that they are an essential part of process that God uses to lead the people who minister to young people in his name towards a greater level of maturity.

On Collaboration (Or, Why God Loves Small Loaves and Scrawny Fish)

A book like this is a collaborative effort and, like any such enterprise, it works best when each member of the team contributes according to his or her particular gifting and experience. At this point in my life, my time is spent studying theology and so I would like to contribute a theological reflection on some of the questions raised by the stories we have read. In particular, I would like to try to draw ideas from a wide range of Christian thinkers, Roman Catholic and Protestant, and see if their concepts might be useful for helping us to make sense of the contributors' questions and experiences, and for suggesting new ways of engaging in youth ministry.

As those who have contributed stories to this volume have shown themselves to be fearless innovators and brave pioneers, a safe piece of theology would seem out of place. So, it is my intention here to stick my head above the parapet and challenge the established limits of our theological thinking. Of course, I do not for a moment think that I, or the theologians I draw upon, have *the* answers. However, I do hope that the fresh perspectives they offer might nudge us towards *better* answers than those we hold today. Fortunately, I believe in a God who delights in taking our measly contributions (small loaves and scrawny fish) and turning them into something life-giving and strengthening. So, in the spirit of the boy with the packed lunch, in the rest of this chapter I would like us to consider the potential impact on our youth ministry practice of fresh perspectives on three important subjects: Christ's mission; the Holy Spirit's work; and what it is to be human.[1]

A Disclaimer

A piece of thinking without limits does require that I make it clear from the outset that while I will be quoting from various contributors and, to some extent, building my reflection around their words and experiences, they might not agree with what I have to say. So, let them be exonerated henceforth from any responsibility for what follows. It's my head above the parapet and any missiles (hopefully of the metaphorical kind) should be directed at me!

On the Mission of Christ (Or, Why the Cross Doesn't Say it All)

If I do get in trouble and have to dodge a few bullets (metaphorically remember) then I'm guessing its going to be here that the trouble starts. Not only does my subtitle call into question the lyrics of one of Christendom's favourite songwriters but (only marginally more importantly) I am going to suggest that it is possible to focus too closely and talk too much of the cross of Christ. As I can already here those metaphorical pistols being cocked I will press on and try to explain why this isn't necessarily heresy …

In his chapter about the work on a Birmingham estate Tim Evans wrote about the failure of his local inner-city church to cope with a damaged young person. The church's error was to think, "surely all he needed was Jesus and everything would be all right." (p. 121) Unfortunately, as we learned, it wasn't all right with Jack. Gary Bishop recognised a similar weakness in his own ministry method when he first arrived in Manchester:

> *I used to think that mission was all about evangelism and converts, I used to think that my goal for each young person was plain and simple conversion and my programs were based around that assumption; every week I would find a new and creative way to communicate the gospel, as I understood it, and lay down a challenge for people to become Christians.*

Now, if you're really alert you will no doubt be jumping up and down on your sofa just now, desperate to point out to any innocent passer-by that neither Evans nor Bishop mentioned the cross. A good point; well made. But in my experience, most formulaic, one-dimensional presentations of the Gospel are closely linked with an overemphasis on the cross of Christ in comparison with the rest of his mission. They cut right to the chase by using a kind of pseudo-logic to move through a rapid series of steps based on Bible verses – all humans have sinned; you're a human, therefore you've sinned; the results of sin are suffering, death and eternal punishment … BUT Jesus suffered and died on a cross in your place; your sins can be forgiven and you'll be saved to life everlasting if only you repent. Now those are genuine biblical truths and in one sense one can but say hallelujah, but these are presentations in a hurry (the fast-food style, McGospel perhaps).

And, at least on my reading, chapter after chapter of this book showed that, particularly beyond the fringe of the church, among the broken and the marginalised, such intellectually-based, cross-focused presentations lacked the power to change lives.

Fortunately, potential answers to the problem were also hinted at in the stories we have read. As his chapter progressed, Evans wrote about *shalom* and its place at the heart of his understanding of the mission. Vitally, he wrote: "The *shalom* of God's Kingdom is most fully expressed in and experienced through the life, teaching, death and rising again of Jesus Messiah (the Christ)." Here the death of Christ is seen against the background of a more holistic view of his mission – not just dying but living, teaching and rising too. This broader emphasis is vital if we are to be able to value every part of the work of a *Church Unlimited* as it takes good news to those who need it. In particular, I think we need to emphasise the "living" part of the mission of Christ.

Some theologians, far from the evangelical position, see the very fact of the eternal Logos of God coming and *living* in a fallen world as being the essential aspect of the salvific mission of Christ, far more important than his *dying* on a cross. Such theologians emphasise the fact that at the Fall all of creation suffered a terrible reversal. A "wrongness" that was deeper and wider than mere human sin entered the world and affected everything. The whole of creation and not simply the human individual was alienated from God.

However, when the Logos of God, through whom the universe was created, entered that fallen universe, his material presence began to put things right. The sun was changed as its light fell upon the tanned skin of the physical manifestation of the divine Son of God. The fruit of the earth was altered as its substance passed his lips and was turned into energy-for-living in his stomach. The possibilities for wholesome human relationships were re-written as he sat and ate, laughed and cried with men and women he called friends. With Christ *in* it a new kind of being became possible for creation. Paul, writing to the Colossians, describes Christ's cosmic mission in this way:

> *He [Christ] is the image of the invisible God, the firstborn over all creation. For by him all things were created: things in heaven and on earth, visible and invisible, whether thrones or powers or rulers or authorities; all things were created by him and for him. He is before all things, and in him all things hold together ... For God was pleased to have all his fullness dwell in him, and through him to reconcile to himself all things, whether things on earth or things in heaven, by making peace through his blood, shed on the cross.*
> (Colossians 1 vs 15-17 and 19-20)

Ah, you're jumping up and down on your sofa again. Because yes, yes, I know, Paul finishes with an emphasis on *the cross*. But now, if we see the importance of the whole mission of Christ, as a cosmic mission, as one where his coming, living, teaching, dying and rising are *all* important, then we see the cross in its proper context and perspective. We might talk quantitatively less about the cross but, qualitatively, it means so much more – the cross becomes more, not less, amazing and more, not less, powerful.

So, what difference might this broadening of the focus of our understanding of Christ's mission have on the actual day-to-day outworking of our Christian faith with and among young people? Returning to the contributors, it is interesting to note that Pete Brierley sees the mission he and his church are engaged in this way:

> *Responding to the local need is at the core of who we are as a church. John tells us "the word became flesh and dwelt among us." We must dwell in our communities and through our living we must bring about God's Kingdom, shalom, fullness of life to all that we meet, whether Muslim*

or Jew, male or female, rich or poor, young or old.

If we see Jesus' coming into the world and living under the conditions of existence just as we do (with all the physical and emotional discomforts, embarrassments, joys and pains that that entails) as an essential part of his salvific mission, then we will see our living alongside young people as not merely a precursor to hitting them with that McGospel presentation but as being, in its own right, the offering of the Gospel and the possibility of salvation. We model ourselves on Christ and recognising the importance of the thirty years that he lived in the fallen world before he began his ministry, then of the three years that he spent preaching the kingdom of God and healing people of physical sufferings, ennobles and makes significant every moment spent alongside young people, and even hints at the salvific potential of the healing that that being-with brings.

On the Holy Spirit's Work (Or, What the West Can Learn from the East)

In the course of doing some research for this and other projects, I have recently come across a number of stories of youth ministries that were birthed in the charismatic, Holy Spirit revival of the late-sixties and early-seventies.

One couple, who had run Methodist class meetings since they were first married, told me of the way the testimony of a member of their group led them to begin their own search for the empowering filling of the Holy Spirit. When they found what they were looking for and experienced God in a new way it led to the transformation of their Christian lives and, eventually, to the foundation of an incredibly successful youth group called "Open Circle". They assured me that the magnetism that drew more and more young people to the group was the remarkable love and passion poured out on the young people by the Holy Spirit. In this book, Father

Dermot Donnelly writes of how the Hexham and Newcastle Youth Ministry Team was born out of the Roman Catholic Charismatic Renewal.

I have been really encouraged by these stories of the Holy Spirit at work in the Church. However, I think that in the charismatic movement in particular (and I'd consider myself part of that movement) it's easy to come to think of the Holy Spirit as, in some sense, our possession – a special blessing that enlivens our relationship with God, and/or a special anointing of power given us by God to enable us to do his work.

This lazy thinking often goes hand-in-hand with the temptation to draw us-and-them distinctions between the spirited "goodies" in the church and the spirit-less "baddies" (or "lost", "unsaved", "pagans") outside the church. How many times do our God-slots, evangelistic talks and sermons begin by painting a blacker-than-black picture of godless living outside the church before launching into an unfeasibly positive and upbeat account of Christian life in the Spirit within the church?

If, though, we choose to take the time to think clearly and look honestly, we would have to admit that there is much of life, light and love outside the church while much darkness persists within. How many times has the worldwide church been dragged kicking and screaming towards the truth by supposedly secular forces? In the last century the stories of women's liberation, of apartheid, and of concern for the environment provide three challenging examples of the outside world leading the church. The unpleasant reality of child abuse within our churches is an equally challenging example of an area where darkness has persisted on the inside. How can we make sense of this paradox: stubborn pockets darkness even within the church, where the Holy Spirit reigns; and bursts of light outside in the world, where we seem to expect only darkness? I think this problem is related to our long history of lazy thinking with regard to the work of the Spirit.

Dramatic divorces and sudden splits are staples of gossip magazines and websites. Unfortunately, the history of our beloved Church has its fair share of meticulously documented divorces and partings. From the local level, to the denominational, to the international we have not always managed to show the love for one another that Jesus said would be the mark of his disciples.

The biggest split of all occurred nearly 1,000 years ago when the churches of the East, which we now know as the Orthodox churches, divided from the Roman Catholic church of the West. Inevitably such divisions involve personal power-plays, political intrigues and Machiavellian machinations, but if we set those aside for a moment there was one particular *theological* reason for the split and it had to do with the relation of the Holy Spirit to Jesus Christ.

Without wanting to delve too deep into what is known as the *filioque* controversy, we can roughly say that the churches of the West saw the Spirit's role as being in some way subservient to the mission of the Son, Jesus Christ. Meanwhile, the Orthodox churches of the East argued that the Holy Spirit was directly related to the Father and had his own role and mission that overlapped with and related to that of the Son but that wasn't contained or limited by it.

So, for a thousand years the church, from which everyone writing in this book (whether Protestant or Roman Catholic) is descended, has held a theology that primarily sees the Spirit as the Spirit of Christ, rather than as the Spirit of God (the Father) more generally. Inevitably, this leads to the assumption that the real work of the Spirit takes place where Christ is preached and people gather in his name – i.e. in the church. It is this millennia-long tradition that makes it so easy for us to think lazily that the Spirit is "ours".

However, in the last fifty years there has been a great increase in ecumenical dialogue between the churches of the East and those of the West and, as a result, a number of Western theologians have been struck by the way their Eastern counterparts understand the Holy Spirit. In the East, where the Spirit is seen primarily as the Spirit of the Father, or as the Spirit of life in general, there is a far higher expectation of seeing the Holy Spirit at work all over creation and throughout all human cultures and societies. And it can be argued that this is far closer to the Spirit as understood by Judaism from the writings of the Old Testament.

OK, so that's the (ancient) history, now let's see if we can drag ourselves back into the present and the practical implications of all of that for our youth ministry. A number of the contributors to this book seem to speak of God as present and at work by his Spirit even before the Christian ministers arrive. With regard to the church in Openshaw, Gary Bishop writes:

> *My personal belief is that amidst all the debris, God's kingdom is already here, sown into the fabric of the land and into the lives of our neighbours and friends, and our job is simplyto point out, uncover and explain the wonder of God as he appears all around us.*

Chris Russell speaks of:

> *This radical notion that we aren't just bringing God into a situation, a place, a group of people from which he has been absent, but are actually asking him to open up our eyes to see what he has been up to, what he has been uncovering, what he has been making possible, and what he intends to do.*

If we set aside our lazy thinking and draw upon what the Eastern church can teach us, we can see that this isn't just rose-spectacled romanticism but an entirely orthodox and biblical way of understanding the work of the Spirit.

Again, we must ask, how should this affect the way we think about and go about our task of being the church to, with and alongside young people? First, I think it should radically change our default position towards what is occurring outside the church. Of course there is sin and deception outside of the church (as, unfortunately, there is sin and deception inside) but there is also the Spirit. Whenever individuals, agencies or societies are working to bring a measure of hope, healing or wholeness to young people we should be prepared to recognise that the Holy Spirit is at work. We should be willing to work in partnership with our "secular" counterparts even as they, perhaps unknowingly, are working in partnership with the Spirit of life. Secondly, as the contributors I have quoted above suggest, we should be looking for God's presence and work in young people's lives and cultures even when the name of Christ is unacknowledged or even unknown. This is essential if, as Nick Shepherd writes in his introductory chapter, we are to find our place in the *missio Dei* rather than just doing our own thing and expecting "our" Holy Spirit to fire us up.

On What It Is to Be Human (Or, Why God's "Yes" Trumps the Theologians' "No")

Writing about the Superkidz project on the Ferrier estate in London, Helen Russell tells of how she decided to invite a couple of the children's mothers to join the organizing team.

> *On one occasion, two mums who were deeply moved during a listening prayer team training session, described in non-church language how Jesus had spoken to them. Such opportunities would have been totally missed if we had adhered to a strict "Christian-only" team policy.*

How do we make sense of non-Christians being spoken to by God? Aren't non-believers cut off from God by their un-repented, un-forgiven sins? Isn't that what we have always been taught?

Haven't we all seen the Gospel illustrations that emphasise the impassable chasm or the insurmountable barrier that separate us from God before we are "saved"? Were the mums and, by implication, the Superkidz team, mistaken?

I think not. If we are to understand what happened in the Superkidz prayer meeting we need to remember that, as we discussed in the last section, the Holy Spirit is not restricted to work amongst members of the church. Secondly, we need to re-think a common Christian misrepresentation of what it means to be human, even in a sinful fallen world.

Most (but not all, see below) of the churches and organisations that are represented in this book are expressions of Protestant Christianity. More narrowly, they are expressions of Reformed Protestant Christianity. That is, these churches, and the parachurch organisations that grow out of them, are rooted in the theology of the great Reformer John Calvin. Of all the theological ideas that Calvin's thought bequeathed to the Christian churches that came after him, one of the most powerful is the idea that through a historical fall and personal sin, the image of God in humans and the possibility of human relationship with God are totally destroyed. Until Christ is preached and his salvation is accepted in repentant faith, there is no chance of a link between the perfect, holy God and sinful humans (beyond the outworking of a general divine providence that keeps the world from total dissolution).

This idea is such a strong plank of Reformed theology that the friendship of two theologians, who are among the most celebrated of Calvin's twentieth-century descendents, was destroyed when one of the two (Emil Brunner) dared to suggest that there might be even the tiniest capacity in the sinful human person to at least receive God's message of love and forgiveness when it was offered. "Nein!" screamed Karl Barth. (And that was just the title of the short but vitriolic book he wrote in reply to Brunner!) Between the heavens and earth there is a total and unbridgeable chasm – the non-Christian is completely and utterly cut-off from God.

Generally, this is the tradition in which we have been nurtured but is there another way of understanding the relation of God to the human person who has not yet come to repentance and faith in Christ?

It is by no means coincidental that in this book the most radically different understanding of the situation is offered by a Roman Catholic, Father Alan Michael. In the opening paragraphs of his chapter he asks the question, "How do we help our disaffected youth to explore and discover their spiritual being, and to grow in their experience of the sacred?" Here we see a different viewpoint, one that sees young people as always and already having a spirituality and an experience of the sacred. Our role is to help them to develop this towards the fullness of relationship with God through Christ. Father Alan continues, "What I saw before me were spiritual beings that were locked in on themselves, youngsters full of life but not knowing how to express themselves fully or appropriately."

Again, I want to be careful not to put words into Father Alan's mouth or imply that my thoughts are in his head. Nonetheless, I think that his approach does reflect a view of the human person that assumes that the young people we reach out to are always and already in some kind of relationship with their creator, albeit a relationship that is fractured and distorted by personal sin and the general fallenness of our world.

Actually, there are hints of similar understandings in the writing of other contributors who are not, as far as I know, from a Roman Catholic tradition. For example, Pete Brierley writes:

> *I believe that every one of the young people we work with experiences God in some small way, and I believe every one of them worships him whether its in the songs they*

> *sing, the dances they choreograph or the football they play. They may not know it but they're sat at the table eating the feast and sooner or later they're gonna wake up and ask: 'who's the host?'*

Along similar lines, Chris Russell invites us to look back behind the sad facts of sin and fall and base our understanding of young people on the far more foundational and important fact of their having been created by a loving God in his image.

> *My theology of humanity is rooted in Genesis 1 rather than Genesis 3 … Surely our first word on humanity should be: "God's verdict on everyone is the same; we are made in his image and for his glory, we are objects of his love and salvation, and when we live in relationship with him we discover who we are made to be."*

Once again, if we allow our understandings to be challenged and perhaps brought back into balance by the insights of those outside of our traditions we can radically re-think the nature and practice of our work with young people.

On this account the decision to invite "non-Christians" onto the Superkidz team is entirely justified. The fact that in the context of a prayer meeting they themselves were able to hear from God is entirely understandable. In the prayer meeting they might not have heard the Gospel preached, they might not have been offered the chance to repent of their sins or accept Christ as Saviour and Lord, but they were certainly shown how a Christian's relationship with God is far less fractured and distorted because of what Christ has done. They didn't have good news intellectually explained but they had it modelled for them. Unsurprisingly, and wonderfully, they didn't respond intellectually either, they responded in kind – by reflecting back what it means to be in relationship with Christ. What a radical and inspiring model of giving and receiving the Gospel!

Post-Postscript (Or, Why Salvation Might Not Equal Conversion)

I opened this postscript with a header taken from Paul's first letter to Timothy and I'll repeat a few phrases from those verses here. We labour for "the living God, who is the saviour of all humanity, especially those who believe." At the close of this postscript and therefore of this book, I would like to wonder aloud about that verse for a few lines.

I wonder whether we might be able to combine that verse with some of the fresh understandings of Christ's mission, the Spirit's work and of the human person that we have just discussed in a way that dissolves the difference between projects that are focused on the "earthly" salvation of young people and projects that are based on their "eternal" salvation. (In practice, I believe that many of the projects featured in this book have already done *precisely* that.)

Again, I will turn to the words of the contributors to support my wondering, even while I reiterate that they might not agree with me! I think that Jo Dolby of One Eighty should be celebrated as the contributor most determined to focus our thoughts on the need for relevant but explicit preaching of the Gospel. She writes:

> *I am passionate about One Eighty the evangelistic outreach; reaching relevantly, preaching the Word of God and seeing young people connect back to God for the rest of eternity.*

That every young person should enjoy the bliss of that eternity in relationship with God would, I believe, be the goal of every other contributor too, regardless of the exact place of their ministry on the evangelism-to-social-action spectrum. Those working in many and varied projects on the Ferrier estate put it like this:

> *Whilst the definitive fulfilment of my vision is for people to*

know Jesus as Saviour through our Gospel-based work, I believe that those who partake of the Kingdom of God through new opportunities and released potential experience something of eternal significance that cannot ultimately leave them untouched.

To paraphrase Paul, the dwelling-with in the midst of brokenness; the healing of past wounds emotional, physical and spiritual; the opening-up of new horizons and possibilities for life is a bringing of salvation from the living God. Given that, as we have seen, this kind of salvation is also based in the mission of Christ to be in and to mend a broken world, in the work of the Holy Spirit outside of the church, and in the relation of every human person to their creator, there is reason to hope and believe that this kind of salvation has eternal significance. Nonetheless, to stay with Paul, we continue to believe that there is a "special" joy in the salvation that comes through an intentional, devoted and Spirit-filled relation to God through Christ lived out as part of his people on earth – the *Church Unlimited*.

Note

1 If there are any theology-nerds out there, I'll put that into academic-speak and reveal my sources – we'll be looking at a Christology/soteriology flavoured by Paul Tillich; a pneumatology a la Jurgen Moltmann; and a theological anthropology that nods towards Karl Rahner.

APPENDIX

Your Contribution to Church Unlimited

It is our sincere hope that the stories in this book have proved to be inspirational and challenging. It may be that you are working in a context where the experiences, struggles, insights and vision of our contributors have enabled you to re-imagine your role and work. It may be however, that though you share similar circumstances with our authors – their determination, their dedication has left you somehow feeling that your story is one of disappointment. Perhaps your circumstances are such that engagement in ministry with young people outside the church is minimal, or may be your 'church youth group' has itself over the years become more of an 'open youth club' bringing with this fresh problems and opportunities.

Whatever your circumstances, we have tried throughout the book to provide reflection questions that might enhance your interaction with the stories of the vision, joy and struggles our contributors have for a church unlimited. We hope that these have enabled you to reflect on your experience, your opinion and also begin to evaluate your own practice as co-workers (paid or unpaid) in God's mission.

However, we would like to encourage you to reflect a little further so in this appendix we would like to invite you to articulate <u>your story</u> and then re-read it as if were the final contribution to this book. To help you do this we have included 'the brief' which we sent to all of those who contributed. We would like you to write your story along these lines (being as fluid with the brief as some of our contributors perhaps!!). There are several blank pages in this appendix for you to do so – but perhaps you might like to sketch it out in rough first!

Having written your story, we invite you to reflect on it using some of the questions we have posed at the end of the other contributions. This isn't a full blow 'theological reflection' and we would encourage you to engage in a deeper analysis and aim setting process if you wanted to implement your reflections (see resources at end of appendix). However, these are the questions we encourage you to begin with to examine how you contribute and might further still enable a church unlimited…

- Does my ministry connect with young people 'beyond the walls of the church'?

- Do I help young people in my context to connect with their peers?

- Where do I sense a longing to involve myself in a more community focussed mission?

- What might be my next step to acting on this?

- Where is my church active in moving beyond the comfortable in terms of youth ministry?

- What are the dangers/difficulties in trying to stretch our activity beyond this?

- What does my story say about the focuses and biases of my theology?

- How might I strengthen and widen my understanding?

The Brief

We would like you to tell your story, focussing on how being church drives your youth ministry. We want to capture the creativity your project shows and the grace God has given it. Please don't get hung up on our tag lines and descriptions. Simply write about what you're doing; where it is hard and where it is joyful; where it is growing and where it is frustrating. Our suggestion is that you structure your piece in the following way:

Obvious facts and overview [500]
Where in the world are you?
Who is involved with your work?
How long have you been in existence (for this example not you personally)?
Who are the young people you work with?

Account and anecdotes [1000-1500]
How did your project come into life?
What is the essence of what you are trying to achieve?
What do you do in the nuts and bolts of your project?
How does your project interface with the other expressions of church linked to you?

What significant stories could you write about that link to these three questions?

Vision and vulnerability [1,000-1500]
Take a little bit more time to articulate your vision for your ministry. What (or who) has inspired you? Do you have any particular ethos or understanding of church and mission behind your project you would like to articulate?

We also want to encourage honesty. Where are the weaknesses in what you are doing? Where do you think you are vulnerable and how has God sustained you or what are you still longing for?

Over to you...

Thank you – now take time to re-reread your story and go through the reflection questions. If you are willing perhaps you could post both your story and reflections at http://www.youthwork.co.uk/community/ – follow the links and have a good conversation!

If you want to take 'theological reflection' on your work further Laurie Green's (1990) *Let's Do Theology*, is an excellent and detailed introduction to the subject. Robert Beckford's (2004) *God and the Gangs* has a summary of how to undertake structured theological reflection and is also particularly good for examining youth ministry in urban settings. If you want further training our own, What Every Youth Leader Needs to Know course is the perfect introduction and confidence booster. For more fulsome training, the Engage course is also a very helpful structured way of enhancing your understanding and practice and is especially suited to volunteer leaders who as of yet have no formal qualifications (http://www.centreforyouthministry.ac.uk/engage.html). For a web based training approach of similar quality there is the Emerge academy resources (http://www.emergeacademy.net/). Web sites correct at time of going to press. Other training might also be available through your denominational youth officers or networks.

Youthwork the partnership – The Initiatives

Youthwork the Partnership

ALOVE (The Salvation Army for a new generation), Oasis, Spring Harvest, Youth for Christ and Youthwork magazine are working together to equip and resource the church for effective youthwork and ministry.

The partnership exists to offer support, encouragement and ideas for busy youth workers including:

Youthwork the conference

Youthwork the conference is a weekend event designed for church-based volunteer youth workers, with specific streams for younger leaders and salaried youth workers. *Youthwork the conference* has been designed to give training and support by offering encouragement, ideas and resources to busy youth workers. There is also an additional early day conference specifically for full time youth workers.

The conference includes: Main plenary sessions with teaching, worship, prayer, reflection and encouragement plus many practical and skills based seminars covering a wide range of youthwork issues. There is also opportunities to network with others; space to reflect and pray, and access to a large range of youth ministry specialist agencies via an extensive exhibition and resource area.

Youthwork the conference takes place each November. Visit www.youthwork.co.uk/conference or call 0870 060 3327 for more information.

Youthwork the conference is administrated by Spring Harvest.

Youthwork magazine

Since 1992, *Youthwork magazine* has been the magazine of choice for youth workers across the UK. Every issue is packed with resources, information and opinion, providing youth workers with all the latest news on youth ministry and youth culture. Each month there are book, cd and resource reviews, challenging and inspiring articles, Jobsearch, must-see websites, and a pull-out section packed with ready-to-use curriculum resources including drama, discussion triggers, and ways to use music and film with your group. With all this and more jammed into every issue, it's no surprise that so many youth workers consider *Youthwork magazine* essential reading.

On sale in most Christian bookshops. Visit www.youthwork.co.uk/magazine or call 01892 652364 for more information or to subscribe.

Youthwork magazine is published by CCP Limited.

Youthwork the resources

A series of books to help youth workers in their youthwork and ministry, in three categories. 'Developing Practice' titles are designed for all those engaged in youthwork and ministry. They are inspirational and practical without being overtly theoretical. 'Challenging Thinking' titles are designed for those who are serious about youthwork and ministry. They are sometimes controversial, always challenging, but never dogmatic. 'Resourcing Ministry' titles provide busy youth workers with tried and tested ideas and curriculum to use with their young people.

Visit www.youthwork.co.uk/resources or call 01825 769111 for more information.

Youthwork the resources are published by Spring Harvest Publishing.

Youthwork the training

What Every Volunteer Youth Worker Should Know

A training course for busy 'extra timers' who need to know the basics – and fast! This innovative course provides a foundation of knowledge, tips and resources in an accessible and practical format. The course is made up of 9 two-hour sessions which may be delivered in a variety of ways to fit needs and lifestyle! You can choose when and where you do the sessions. Participation includes a free resource book and 100 ready-to-use ideas. The course is endorsed by a broad spectrum of Christian denominations and networks.

Visit www.youthwork.co.uk/training/volunteerscourse or call 0207 450 9044 for more information.

'What Every Volunteer Youthworker Should Know' is managed and delivered by Oasis.

The Art of Connecting

A resource to equip you and your youth group to see lives changed... forever! The vision behind 'The Art of Connecting' is the realisation that people communicate most naturally when they are exploring their own stories together. The course aims to empower people to share their faith through story – making connections between their story, their friends' stories and God's story.

'The Art of Connecting' book and Leaders Pack are available, as are regional training days for youth leaders and young people.

Visit www.youthwork.co.uk/training/aoc or call 0121 550 8055 for more information.

'The Art of Connecting' is developed and delivered by Youth for Christ.

Youthwork online

www.youthwork.co.uk features a dynamic home page updated weekly with the latest information, news analysis and views on youthwork and youth culture – all things that will be of interest to all those working with young people. It's also the place to find out about the partnership and how we can support you, including more details on the conference, magazine, training courses, and resources, and access to the Youthwork online directory.

At www.youthwork.co.uk/community there is a range of online discussion forums with discussions on youth ministry issues, plus forums to share and resources with other youth workers from across the country.

Visit www.youthwork.co.uk for more information.

Youthwork online is owned by CCP Limited and developed by all the partners.

Youthwork the partnership – The Partners

Oasis

Oasis develops effective ways of transforming the lives of the poor and marginalised and whole communities in the UK and around the world. We help churches and individuals do the same.

Drawing on 20 years experience of pioneering mission, education and youth work initiatives; Oasis provides opportunities for young people to participate in life changing UK and Global mission on both a short and long term basis and equips youth workers with innovative resources and training including the 'What Every Volunteer Youth Worker Should Know' course & the JNC-qualifying Oasis Youth Work and Ministry Degree.

Oasis also enables youth workers and church volunteers to support young people's personal, social and health education in their local schools through training associate educators in Sex and Relationships Education and Mentoring as well as tackling social exclusion among young people head on through the delivery of one to one transition work, mentoring and supported housing programmes.

To find out more:
Visit: www.oasistrust.org
Email: enquiries@oasistrust.org
Phone: 0207 450 9000
Write to: Oasis, The Oasis Centre, 115 Southwark Bridge Road, London SE1 0AX, England.

ALOVE

The Salvation Army for a new generation

ALOVE

ALOVE is The Salvation Army for a new generation. ALOVE is calling a generation to dynamic faith, radical lifestyle, adventurous mission and a fight for justice.

ALOVE provides young people and young adults with ongoing opportunities to engage in culturally engaging worship, cell and small group discipleship, innovative mission and world changing social action.

ALOVE runs training programmes to develop leaders and missionaries for the 21st century. ALOVE is also pioneering new expressions of church, youth work and social inclusion in communities around the United Kingdom and Ireland.

To find out more about ALOVE:
Visit: www.salvationarmy.org.uk/ALOVE
Email: ALOVE@salvationarmy.org.uk
Phone: 0208 288 1202
Write to: ALOVE UK, The Salvation Army, 21 Crown Lane, Morden, Surrey, SM4 5BY, England.

Spring Harvest

Spring Harvest's vision is to 'equip the Church for action'. Through a range of events, conferences, courses and resources we enable Christians to impact their local communities and the wider world.

Spring Harvest is probably best known for Main Event, held every Easter, which attracts over 55,000 people of all ages. Over 10,000 of those attending are young people. The Main Event also includes specific streams which cater for over 2,000 students. Alongside the teaching programme, Spring Harvest provide a range of resources for young people and those involved in youth ministry.

Through our sister company – Spring Harvest Holidays – we offer quality holidays at our four-star holiday park in the Vendee, France. These inspirational holidays cater for people of all ages in a safe, secure and relaxed environment.

The Spring Harvest range of resources – albums, books and teaching resources – all aim to equip the Church for action.

To find out more about Spring Harvest:
Visit: www.springharvest.org
Email: info@springharvest.org
Phone: 01825 769000
Write to: Spring Harvest, 14 Horsted Square, Uckfield,
East Sussex, TN22 1QG, England.

Youth for Christ

Youth for Christ (YFC), one of the most dynamic Christian organisations, are taking good news relevantly to every young person in Britain. They help tackle the big issues facing young people today. They're going out on the streets, into schools and communities and have changed the lives of countless people throughout the UK.

Their staff, trainees and volunteers currently reach over 50,000 young people each week and have over 50 centres in locations throughout the UK. They also provide creative arts and sports mission teams, a network of registered groups and a strong emphasis on 'three-story' evangelism. YFC International works in 120 nations.

To find out more about YFC:
Visit: www.yfc.co.uk
Email: churchresource@yfc.co.uk
Phone: 0121 550 8055
Write to: YFC, PO Box 5254, Halesowen,
West Midlands B63 3DG, England.

Youthwork magazine

Youthwork magazine is Britain's most widely read magazine resource for Christian youth workers. Through articles, ready-to-use resources, reviews, youthwork and cultural news and analysis, and much more, Youthwork magazine provides ideas, resources and guidance to help you in your work with young people.

Youthwork magazine is published monthly by CCP Limited, which is part of the Premier Media Group, who also publish Christianity and Christian Marketplace.

To find out more about *Youthwork magazine*:
Visit: www.youthwork.co.uk
Email: youthwork@premier.org.uk
Phone: 01892 652364
Write to: Youthwork Magazine, CCP Limited, Broadway House, The Broadway, Crowborough, TN6 1HQ, England.

Schoolswork.co.uk